Frank Dumont

The Cuban Spy

a Comedy-Drama in four Acts

Frank Dumont

The Cuban Spy
a Comedy-Drama in four Acts

ISBN/EAN: 9783743301511

Manufactured in Europe, USA, Canada, Australia, Japa

Cover: Foto ©ninafisch / pixelio.de

Manufactured and distributed by brebook publishing software
(www.brebook.com)

Frank Dumont

The Cuban Spy

The Cuban Spy

CAST OF CHARACTERS

LITTLE CUBA—"ELINORA" . . *Soubrette—The Cuban Spy*

RICHARD CARSON, a young American aiding
the patriots . . . . *Juvenile comedy*

RODERIGO VALDEZ, secretly in the pay of the
Spaniards . . . . *Heavy*

JASPER GOMEZ }
LOPEZ } officers in Valdez's command, *Second heavy*

PHELIM MCNAB . . . . *Irishman—Irish comedy*

CARL WEISBEER . . . . *Dutch comedy*

JERRY . . . . *Negro comedy*

BRIDGET MONAHAN, who is looking for
Phelim McNab . . . . *Character*

SOPHIE, a waiting maid . . . . *Juvenile*

TIME OF REPRESENTATION, TWO HOURS AND A HALF.

COSTUMES

ELINORA. Act I.—Ragged dress as a stowaway; white waist; hair down; black shoes; 'kerchief about neck. Act II.—Cuban girl, semi-Spanish and very picturesque. Second dress, Spanish costume, veil; short skirts; colored hose and slippers. Act III.—First dress, Sister of Red Cross order, black gown, white cap. Second, Cuban boy, jaunty cap, jacket and short pants. Similar to Spanish bull fighter. Act IV.—Grand evening dress costume; train dress and jewels.

RICHARD CARSON. Semi-military dress; change in remaining acts to business suit. No coat or vest in Act III as prisoner.

VALDEZ. Semi-sea-faring costume in Act I. A partially military costume of Spanish cut for the remaining acts, except Act IV, where all characters dress for evening reception.

JASPER. About the same as Valdez, only more in semi-bandit uniform.

PHELIM. Extravagant Irish make-up, to change during acts.

CARL. Made up stout, funny German costume, to change slightly during progress of play. In last act more genteel.

JERRY. Darkey make-up to suit taste of performer.

LOPEZ. A Spanish guerilla, white duck jacket and pants; straw hat; military accoutrements in all the acts except Act I, wherein he is partially in sailor dress.

BRIDGET. Eccentric Irish woman's costume, to change slightly during acts, and to be very gorgeous in Act IV.

SOPHIE. Waiting maid's costume; short skirts; apron; cap; gaudy waist; etc.

4

PROPERTIES

ACT I.—Good size cannon on a truck and to revolve on a pivot. The butt end of cannon is open to allow a horse pistol to be fired through it. Box; coil of rope; frying pan; large bundle of clothing tied so it can be thrown about; handkerchief; spy glass; briar-wood pipe; rope to bind RICHARD to cannon; broom; small American flag; guns and pistols.

ACT II.—Table; chairs; bottles; glasses; matches; cigarettes; small vial; decanter of liquor (sarsaparilla); lighted candle or lamp; female garments for PHELIM and CARL; pistol; torch; red fire; lycopodium flash torch for flames; rope to bind RICHARD; guns for CARL and PHELIM.

ACT III.—Small table; stools; lighted candle; several bags of straw; five guns; several boxes; stool; lot of chains for prisoners; stuffed stick; rope; revolvers for ELINORA; guns for PHELIM and CARL.

ACT IV.—Handsome furniture; curtains for centre doors; carpet; document for ELINORA; imitation of horse's hoofs (cocoa-nuts and slab of marble); handkerchief; chalk for PHELIM'S face; Cuban flag and American flag for ELINORA, larger Cuban flag for Cubans; loaded revolvers; swords, etc., for battle tableau at climax.

SCENE PLOT

ACT I

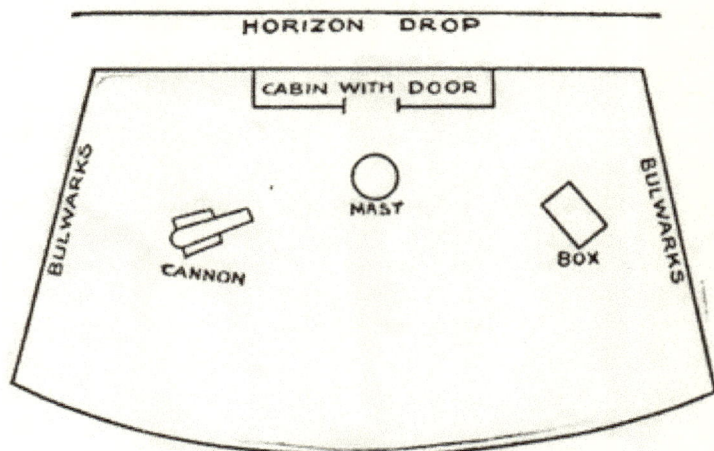

SCENE—Deck of vessel. Horizontal drop at back. Cabin with door in 4th G. Mast, C. Cannon on Pivot, R. Bulwarks, R. and L.

ACT II

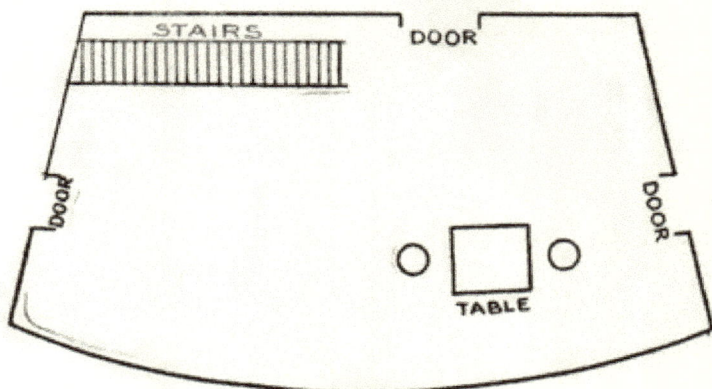

SCENE—Kitchen or plain chamber box set with doors R. and L. Door in flat. Stairs with balustrade, R. U. E. Table and chairs.

Act III

OLD LOG-HOUSE OR PRISON FLATS

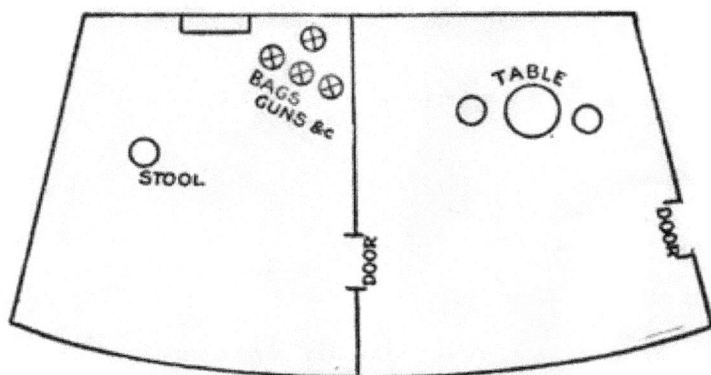

BAGS
GUNS &c

TABLE

STOOL

DOOR

DOOR

SCENE—Interior of old sugar-house (boxed). Stage divided c. Apartments R. and L., with door in dividing partition. Grated window R. in flat, three or four feet from stage. Door, L. Table and old bags and guns.

Act IV

INTERIOR OR GARDEN BACKING

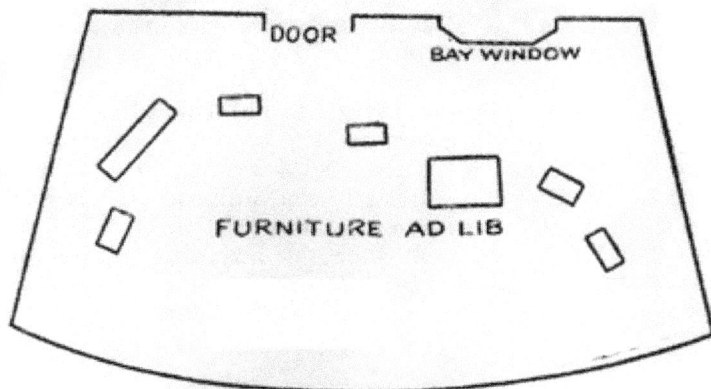

DOOR

BAY WINDOW

FURNITURE AD LIB

SCENE—Handsome parlor (boxed). Door, c., with curtains. Bay window L. flat. Handsome furniture about room.

THE CUBAN SPY

ACT I

SCENE 1.—*Deck of vessel. See diagram for set.*

(*Music. At rise of curtain* JERRY, *the negro cook, discovered with frying pan,* R. BRIDGET MONAHAN *seated on box,* L., *or coil of rope, apparently sea-sick.* JASPER *and a few sailors at rail,* R.)

JERRY. I don't care what you-all think about it, but I say that this vessel is haunted all right, all right. You don't catch me going down in de cellar of this vessel after potatoes any more. I tell you, there's a hoodoo 'round here; may be dat Irish woman, for all I knows.

BRIDGET. Look here, you lump of African bog, don't mention my name through the opening of your face! If I was healthy enough I'd rise up and throw you over the fence of this ship. But I'm so sea-sick that I can't stand on my feet, and it's lucky for you that I can't. Go on! Don't stand there grinning at me like a big, black Tom-cat or I'll forget I'm sick and dance on your neck like I would at Donnybrook fair. Get out of my sight, you nagur! (*Grabs at bundle beside her and throws it at* JERRY.)

JERRY. Here, hold on; don't insult one of the officers of this ship. You're nothing but an ordinary passenger, I'm de head cook and superintendent of de provision department. I'm de sutler, commissary, and food mixer. If I say, "You don't eat," you don't eat. So look out, Irish, or I'll drop a handful of shamrocks in your soup and set you crazy.

JASPER. (*crosses down*) Here, stop all this idle talk. The lady is a passenger and you are the cook of this vessel.

JERRY. I know my place and I knows her place, too. I tell you, you're all "Jonahed" and hoodooed. There's a ghost on this ship, and you can't deny it.

JASPER. Very well. If there is anything wrong we'll ferret it out. Won't we, boys?

SAILORS. Yes. Overboard with the Jonah!

9

JASPER. Take a look through the hold. Be careful of
lights, as we have plenty of powder on board. Don't forget that.

(Sailors exit cabin, R.)

JERRY. Suppose somebody was to drop a cigarette in
dat powder. Phew! wouldn't we go up like sky-rockets.
It makes me almost turn pale to think of it. I'm black in
de face, but I've got a white heart. It's a brave heart, but
I've got a pair of cowardly legs. Once I get on dry land
you don't catch this nigger on water again. I wish I could
catch dat man dat wrote "A Life on de Ocean Wave." I'd
give him a grave in de ocean wid a wave of my razor.

(Enters cabin.)

BRIDGET. To think I'd be such a fool for love. Ah,
love! you've driven me almost crazy, and to make me follow a man over land and water this way. My heart's in
my mouth. Ugh! It ain't my heart, it's something I've
swallowed. *(Buries her face in a handkerchief, rocks and
moans ad lib.)*

JASPER. Should the sailors find any one whom they suspect, it would be sure death. Ignorant, superstitious set,
but we need a rough crew at present. The Americans are
sending arms and ammunition to the Cuban rebels. We
are acting as a blockade-runner, taking arms to Cubans, but
really we are in the pay of the Spanish government. It
pays better, and we get a revenue from both parties. These
infernal Yankees are considered smart, but we're one too
many for them. Spain will get even with them when the
time comes.

(PHELIM MCNAB comes from cabin very sick, L.)

PHELIM. I'm doing nothing but rolling around and
creeping around on my hands and knees. Sure I thought
it was a pleasant ride in a row-boat from Florida to Cuba!
But here I am half dead, and I can't keep my insides from
being outsides. *(At this moment he sees BRIDGET. JASPER
is at rail with glass busy scanning the horizon)* What do I
see? Bridget Monahan, and on this vessel! I'm dead and
buried. What the deuce is she following me around everywhere for? She mustn't see me; I'll skip away from
Master Richard if we reach Cuba. *(Hides behind mast as
BRIDGET looks up.)*

BRIDGET. Oh, Phelim, Phelim, where are you?

PHELIM. I'm where you won't find me. I'll jump overboard before you can grab me.

BRIDGET. To leave me this way! And I'm following you all over just for love.

PHELIM. You're not the only oyster-shell in the basket! (L.)

(CARL WEISBEER, *heard in cabin.*)

CARL. Oh, my! Oh, me! Stop de ship! I want to climb out and walk home! (CARL *staggers out of cabin, and almost falls over* BRIDGET *as he goes,* L.)

BRIDGET. Can't you see where you're going, you sausage-headed Dutchman!

PHELIM. (*behind mast*) Ireland and Germany will have a scrap! I'm referee!

BRIDGET. Don't stand there looking at me! Say something, if you have anything on your mind, out with it—up with it!

CARL. Yes. (*staggers to rail—business of sea-sick*) It's off my mind!

PHELIM. That Dutchman has made me sick! (*Staggers* R., *and business of sick.*)

BRIDGET. Oh! There's a poor man over there who feels bad—I'll go over and console him. (*Goes towards* PHELIM, *and as she talks he avoids her, turns his face away, and replies only in monosyllables.* Are you very ill, my poor man? Sure I didn't see you on this vessel before. Can I do anything for you? I'm always sorry for the sick, so I am! Let me see your face, my poor man! (*As she tries to get a look at him he manages to back away, then goes around the mast, then suddenly staggers sideways into cabin, and disappears, much to* BRIDGET'S *surprise.*) Sure I think the man's crazy! Well, well, once I lay my hands on Phelim McNab he'll never get away from me. I heard he was in Cuba, so I set out on his track. I'm suffering a good bit for him (PHELIM *looks out of cabin*) but he'll pay for it all. I'll make him suffer twice as much!

PHELIM. You will—nit! (*Disappears.*)

BRIDGET. Maybe the poor Dutchman needs consolation!

CARL. No, I don't need constellation; I want a constitution. I'll get some of dot Irishman's vitsky (*starts for cabin.*)

BRIDGET. Hold on there! I want to talk to you!

CARL. I ain't got no time! Funny how womens always bodder a man when he don't want them around. (*Darts into cabin, and bumps into* VALDEZ, *who is entering from it.* CARL *falls backward and rises.*) I beg your puddings! (*Enters cabin.*)

BRIDGET. Ah, Captin dear, but you're a fine man ! You run into that lump of sourkrout as nate as a gossoon would thump a head at Donnybrook ! Say ! Captin dear, I'm sick !

VALDEZ. You look it.

BRIDGET. I feel it. Say, Captin, have you a private bottle that's good for indigestion caused by sea-sickness ?

VALDEZ. No ! Your place is in the cabin, not on deck.

BRIDGET. Is that so ? I wouldn't have known it if you hadn't told me. Sure you're a peacock wid your gold-lace cap and spangles on your clothes. What a long tail our cat's got ! Ah ! Ye Spanish cheroot, you ! If the Americans and the Irish ever get after you they'll clip the feathers off of ye mighty quick.

VALDEZ. Ah ! Bah !

BRIDGET. Don't say bah to me. I'm not a sheep. I'm a little Irish lamb, and you'll not put any mint sauce on me, either. That for you and old Spain ! (*Snaps her finger.*) I'd like to see old Weyley put me in jail. I'd have the whole of Ireland over here in a week.

VALDEZ. Hold your tongue !

BRIDGET. I can't. It's too slippery. And you'll not hold it for me, either. I'll have the last word. I'm a woman, and I never let a man have the last word. I'll—I'll—I'd talk to you some more, but I'm sick. (*Business with handkerchief, and staggers into cabin trying to talk to* VALDEZ.) I'll see you when I can talk.

VALDEZ. I must abandon this life. It is growing dangerous. I can remain in Havana without risk. The papers will secure a vast estate, and none can point to me as the criminal. Don Alvarez trusted me in all things, and even in his will made me his heir in case his only child should die. In an evil moment I removed him and placed the little girl upon a vessel sailing for an American port. It was not my first crime as the cursed brand of the felon was seared in my flesh.

(*Enter* JASPER *from cabin.*)

JASPER. Captain (*salutes*), I have observed the American closely, as you have ordered me. I believe he is a spy, and if so, will stand in our way if we attempt to run this cargo into the hands of the Spanish authorities.

VALDEZ. Well, he is but one American among us all ! You know what to do if he becomes two inquisitive. He is but a passenger, same as the others—but we didn't promise to land them anywhere, did we ?

JASPER. No, I understand ! They are on board, but not

landed yet! Mr. Richard Carson had best keep a quiet tongue in his head—or—

VALDEZ. Or—you'll keep it quiet for him. That's the idea! I'll stroll into the cabin and observe him myself. (*Enters cabin.*)

JASPER. These passengers imagine that they own this vessel, but they'll have a rude awakening before long. (*Noise heard in cabin ; music,* R.)

(ELINORA *rushes from cabin, pursued by sailors ; she eludes them and crosses to* R. C., *sailors* L.)

LOPEZ. A stowaway! We found her concealed in the hold.

JASPER. Let her be secured! (*Sailors rush towards her. She runs towards cabin and into the arms of* RICHARD CARSON, *who enters from it. Sailors start back. Picture.*)

ELINORA. Save me, or they will kill me!

RICHARD. What does this mean? Why do you attack a defenceless girl?

JASPER. She is a stowaway, and she can't remain on this vessel.

SAILORS. Over with the Jonah!

ELINORA. Don't let them kill me, sir. I will leave the vessel if they will but set me adrift upon a spar! Will you protect me?

RICHARD. With my life! He who attempts to harm you will answer to me! You are under my protection!

JASPER. Down with the American if he interferes.

RICHARD. Advance, cowards, advance! but the first who approaches will lie upon this deck. I am an American, and I protect a female in distress wherever I find her!

JASPER. I warn you not to interfere with me or this crew if you value your life.

ELINORA. Do not make enemies of them on my account. Leave me to them. You must not sacrifice your life for mine.

RICHARD. I have faced death too often to allow these curs to frighten me. They may intimidate a woman, but a man is not afraid of such dogs.

JASPER. Surrender! We are all against one.

PHELIM. (*enters from cabin*) That's a lie! You're all against two. I'm in this fight with you, Master Richard. We're two against the lot of 'em.

CARL. (*comes from cabin*) Make it three. I fights mit you against dat gang of snoozers.

JASPER. Down with them! No quarter! Make quick work of it!

(*Music.*—JASPER *and Sailors attack* RICHARD, *who fells* JASPER *to the deck.* CARL *knocks down a sailor, and* PHELIM *levels a briar-wood pipe at them. Sailors fall back.*)

PHELIM. Be gob, but they're afraid of a briar-wood pipe (*laughs*).

(*Enter* VALDEZ *from cabin.*)

VALDEZ. What is the meaning of this tumult?
JASPER. (*who has risen*) We found a stowaway, and that American busybody interfered with us. He struck me, but his life will pay for the blow.
CARL. Ah! blow all you want to. You're a blower from Blowersville.
PHELIM. A fine lot of sailors! Try to murder a woman and then let me bluff them with a pipe. Dutchy, we're the boys to make them dance to our music, ain't we?
CARL. If I play de " Wacht am Rhine " I'll make 'em do de " hitchy kitchy," I bet you.
VALDEZ. (to *Jasper*) Leave all to me. I'll give you a chance to retaliate in a short time. (*Aloud*) Jasper, no more of this unseemly conduct. Take the men forward.
JASPER. All right, Captain.

(JASPER *and Sailors exit,* R. I E.)

PHELIM. German regiment, attention! Fall in! By the right flank! By platoons! Form a hollow square! In a double line! Forward—march!

(*Putting* CARL *into short drill, they exit into cabin, imitating a drum, one singing* "*Yankee Doodle.*")

VALDEZ. (to RICHARD) This is a stowaway and sailors as a rule treat them in a rough manner. I will look into the matter and have my men apologize to you (*aside*) and a solid apology rest assured. (*Enters cabin.*)
ELINORA. Señor, how can I ever repay you for risking your life to save mine?
RICHARD. Do not speak of the matter Danger is past and you are safe. I have simply performed my duty as a man.
ELINORA. Your face and noble action will be engraven upon my heart.

RICHARD. What is your name?

ELINORA. I am called Little Cuba. You are an American, and all Americans are friends of the poor struggling patriots of Cuba. I can therefore trust you. With the aid and friendship of Americans Cuba will be free—free as you are yourselves. You may surmise that I am a spy, and so I am. This vessel, though a blockade runner and apparently taking arms and ammunition to the patriots, is in reality in the hands of a Spanish villain who will allow the Spaniards to take this vessel and cargo if he can. The Captain, while pretending friendship for the Cubans, is really their worst foe. He is a villain!

RICHARD. So I have judged him. We came aboard as passengers to Havana from Key West, and I have seen enough of him to suspect that his crew of ruffians would not hesitate at murder. But tell me, do they suspect you?

ELINORA. I think not, merely taking me for a stowaway or Jonah. I am known as Elinora to all save you. I wish to reach Havana for a certain purpose, and to be of service to Cuba. I hope to aid the brave men who will avenge Maceo's death.

RICHARD. Aye, and to pay back the cowardly curs who basely murdered him. A million Americans will spring to arms if haughty Spain but dares to offer another insult to our flag.

ELINORA. Bravely said, and I know you mean every word of it. The story of my life is a sad one, and would weary you to relate it. I will merely say that my father was murdered by a false friend, and I, a little child, was sent away in the care of hired villains. I managed to escape, and in after years to return to Cuba, only to find the villain in full possession of my father's estates; but he had departed for Spain, and I could prove no claim; I am on the trail of that villain, and I feel that some day I will meet him face to face. (*Crosses to* L.)

RICHARD. Did you ever see him, or note anything peculiar whereby you might identify him?

(VALDEZ *appears at cabin door and listens.*)

ELINORA. On that fatal night I heard my father's cry for help, and rushed to his assistance. I seized the assassin by the arm, and as he threw me aside I saw by a flash of lightning that gleamed through the window, deeply imprinted on the man's hand a letter—the letter A!

(VALDEZ *starts—looks at palm of his hand, and goes behind mast.*)

RICHARD. **That is a clue.** It was the custom years ago in the Spanish settlements to burn a letter upon a criminal's arm, hand, or shoulder.

VALDEZ. 'Tis his child—but I am safe if I can keep this accursed mark hidden. (*Enters cabin.*)

ELINORA. That is my only clue, and a small voice within my heart that bids me hope—watch and wait.

RICHARD. We must leave this vessel before she reaches the island of Cuba! Perhaps we may secure one of the boats, and thus make our escape.

ELINORA. The Captain interfered merely to blind you!

(*Music*—VALDEZ, JASPER *and sailors come from cabin.*)

VALDEZ. There is the stowaway. She is a spy, and you may do with her as you like.

JASPER. Cast her overboard!

SAILORS. Yes—throw her overboard!

RICHARD. Would you murder a defenceless woman?

VALDEZ. I am the captain of this vessel, and will do as I please.

RICHARD. But you won't do as you please with this poor girl now under my protection. Remember I am a passenger, and claim my rights as such.

VALDEZ. I'll hang you from the yard-arm for interfering with me and my orders.

RICHARD. Where is Phelim?

VALDEZ. (*laughs*) Your German and Irish friends are secured below.

BRIDGET. (*at cabin*) If there's any one locked up below, sure I'll unlock 'em again. (*Disappears.*)

VALDEZ. Now, my fine American, you're left to yourself, and I leave you to the tender mercies of my crew.

RICHARD. You are a pirate, a villain! Entrusted with this cargo for the Cubans, you intend to betray them.

VALDEZ. I'll make sure you won't tell any one about it. Seize him! (*Sailors seize* RICHARD.)

RICHARD. You treacherous dog!

VALDEZ. I'd send a bullet through your brain, but I've reserved you for something else. I'll try your nerve; I'll try your American courage; your pluck, if you have any. Do you see that cannon? Bind him to its muzzle. (RICH-ARD *is bound by rope, facing the cannon, the muzzle to his breast.*)

ELINORA. Surely you would not doom him to such a horrible fate. Spare him! Take my life if you will, but be merciful to him. (*Kneels to* VALDEZ.)

RICHARD. Do not kneel to that villain. Arise! I am an American, and I can die in the defence of the downtrodden and for a woman, alone and unprotected. An American defies the cowardly Spanish dogs who yelp and bark at my heels.

VALDEZ. Seize this girl! (*Two sailors seize* ELINORA.) Lopez, to your post!

LOPEZ. Aye, aye, Captain! (*Stands ready to fire cannon.*)

(ELINORA *suddenly breaks from sailors, snatching a revolver from the belt of one, and levels it at* VALDEZ. *Picture.*)

ELINORA. Speak the word to fire that gun and you are a dead man!

PHELIM *and* CARL *come from cabin, armed. Sailors strike up* ELINORA'S *hand. General fight takes place.* PHELIM *attacks* LOPEZ, CARL *attacks* JASPER. BRIDGET *runs on from cabin with a broom and attacks sailors.* LOPEZ *suddenly fights his way to the cannon.* ELINORA *quickly releases* RICHARD *from cannon. Soon as* RICHARD *is out of the way the cannon is fired at* VALDEZ'S *command.* PHELIM *waving small American flag, and on this quick picture*

CURTAIN

ACT II

SCENE.—*Interior of old inn, Matanzas. See scene plot. Music.* LOPEZ, *as landlord of inn, discovered. Several men are seated at table,* R. C.

LOPEZ. The Captain will pay a good price if we succeed. The American carries a quantity of money, and besides, he is not wanted in Cuba.

(*Enter* JASPER, *disguised, door flat.*)

JASPER. Be careful! The American will soon be here. Remember! You are all patriots now. You were never on board of the blockade runner, and above all, do not let him see through our present disguise. Hark! Some one approaches.

(*Enter* BRIDGET, *door* F.)

BRIDGET. What a murdering country and what a lot of homely men! Nose on 'em like badgers and whiskers like a baboon! Sure, if you were in Ireland and St. Patrick was alive he'd drive yees all into the sea for snakes and toads. Talk up, some one of yees, for I'm in the humor for a fight.

LOPEZ. My dear madam, what do you want?

BRIDGET. Is this a hotel or is it a museum?

LOPEZ. It is a hotel.

BRIDGET. Well, I'm glad I know what it is. 'Pon my word I never saw such an ugly lot of men in all my life! But ye can't help it! (*To one of the men*) Does your face hurt you? Why don't you try to wear it upside down? Oh! my! What a face to stamp butter? And there's a man so cross-eyed that he can look into his own ear! Well, if this is a hotel, show me the best room you have in the house.

LOPEZ This way, madam. We will do our best to make you comfortable. (*Bows her out,* R. I E.)

BRIDGET. Oh! what a homely lot of men! They have scrubbing-brushes for whiskers! Oh, my! Oh, my! I hope I won't dream about them! (*Exit,* R. I E.)

JASPER. That gabbling woman may be in our way. I wish Lopez had sense enough to refuse her accommodations. Still, we can easily rid ourselves of such people, if needs be.

18

(*Enter* RICHARD *and* PHELIM, *door,* F.)

RICHARD. Good evening, gentlemen!

JASPER. Good evening!

(PHELIM, *startled by the voice, comes down and circles about* JASPER, *as if to trace a resemblance, etc.*)

PHELIM. I thought I remembered that voice. It belonged to as big a blackguard and cut-throat as ever trod the earth or sailed on a ship—a blockade runner, maybe!

JASPER. Your comparison is not an agreeable one, sir.

PHELIM. And the man I mean wasn't agreeable, either. But no matter. I suppose all Spaniards look alike!

JASPER. What do you mean?

PHELIM. They're mean enough for anything.

(LOPEZ *enters* R. 1 E., *passes by* PHELIM, *who gazes at him intently.*)

LOPEZ. Welcome, gentlemen! Make yourselves at home.

PHELIM. We'll do that, my bucko, whether you want us to or not. Sit down, Master Richard, when in Rome do as the Roman candles do—when in Cuba do as the Cubanians do—and we'll do anybody that tries to do us. (*Sits down and puts his feet on the table.*)

JASPER. (*to* RICHARD) I am always glad to meet Americans. They sympathize with us and aid us at every chance.

RICHARD. We never refuse to extend a helping hand to the cause of liberty. Our Republic is made up of men who sought our shores to escape oppression, and once they breathe the air of freedom they are anxious that all other lands may be as free! I know not if you are a Cuban or a Spaniard, but I will say this to you, my heart is with the struggling Cubans, and I am ready to aid them in their battle against cruel oppression. Every liberty-loving man in the United States thinks as I do.

PHELIM. And in Ireland, too! We're not free ourselves, but we'll get there! Here's to the American eagle and Yankee Doodle that will make that yaller-faced Weyler "walk Spanish" if he tries a bluff on us, now.

JASPER. I'm glad to meet you both; we need aid and the services of brave men. We are all patriots and we're friends of the cause.

RICHARD. I am pleased to meet you! There is such a thing as pretending to be friendly to Cuba and betraying those who risk their lives in her cause.

JASPER. That is very true, we live in troublous times.
(*Whistle heard.*) Here comes one who has been outlawed
for his devotion to Cuba, Señor Rial. (*Enter* VALDEZ, L. I
E. *He is thoroughly disguised.*) Señor Rial, I wish you to
meet this brave American—he is one of us in heart and
intentions.

VALDEZ. Señor American, I am proud to meet you!
(*Shakes hands.*)

PHELIM. And I'm Phelim McNab! You're Señor Rial,
and I'm the "rale" thing! I think that I have met you
before.

VALDEZ. That is hardly possible. I am a native of this
isle and have never visited your country!

PHELIM. You may not have been in Ireland but I think
you've been on the water!

VALDEZ. (*laughs*) I am not a sailor.

PHELIM. But you might be a cruiser, a blockade runner,
or a sort of a pirate.

VALDEZ. Sir! I will not brook an insult.

PHELIM. Keep your shirt on! I said you looked it. If
the cap fits you you can wear it.

RICHARD. Phelim, the subject is not a pleasant one to
Señor Rial.

PHELIM. Maybe it's too "real" for him. Well, I've
spoke my mind and that's all there is about it. It's not my
fault if he looks like a black-muzzled pirate or a rapscallion,
is it? Sit down "Real" and put a piece of ice on your
cocoa-nut to keep your brains cool.

VALDEZ. (*to* RICHARD) I will not notice your eccentric
friend. I do not understand his style of joking.

PHELIM. You'll see the joke later on.

(*Enter* ELINORA *disguised as a Cuban girl. She comes over
to table, is surprised to see* RICHARD.)

VALDEZ. Come, Lopez! Bring us some of your choice
wine, mind you, none of your cheap red vinegar—but the
real juice of grapes.

(ELINORA *starts at the voice, but lights a cigarette by scratch-
ing a match upon the bald part of* PHELIM'S *head.* LOPEZ
exits.)

PHELIM. Hold on there! What do you take my skull
for? A bit of sandpaper or the side of a match-box?

ELINORA. Señor will please excuse me, I am very near-
sighted.

PHELIM. Well! Well. She's that near-sighted she didn't know I had a head on me. Well, I accept your apology, but don't do it again.

(LOPEZ *returns with bottle of wine and glasses. Places it on table. Pours out wine.* VALDEZ *unobserved pours contents of small vial into* RICHARD'S *glass.* ELINORA *sees the action.*)

VALDEZ. Here is to our cause, and may it prove successful! (*As* RICHARD *is about to drink* ELINORA *spills his wine, then pretends it was an accident.*)

ELINORA. Oh! excuse me. I am so near-sighted.

VALDEZ. (*aside*) Confounded meddler! (*Rises and goes to* ELINORA.) Who are you?

ELINORA. I am myself, who are you?

VALDEZ. Answer; where did you come from?

ELINORA. Outside.

VALDEZ. How did you get in here?

ELINORA. Through the door. I couldn't drop down through the chimney, could I? (*Blows smoke into* VALDEZ'S *face.*)

VALDEZ. None of your insolence! What do you want here?

ELINORA. Nothing. Have you got it?

VALDEZ. I'll wring your neck for you.

ELINORA. No, you won't. I don't care that for you! (*Snaps finger at him.*) I'm not afraid of you.

VALDEZ. A still tongue makes a wise head!

ELINORA. Then you'll never be wise. You talk too much!

VALDEZ. What was your object in striking that gentleman's wine glass?

ELINORA. Merely an accident, I assure you. It was fit to drink, wasn't it? You wouldn't do anything crooked, would you?

VALDEZ. I'd like to know who and what you are!

ELINORA. You'd like to know who and what I am. I am a Cuban. So are you, ain't you? We are both fighting for a cause. Mine is a good one. I don't know about yours. Are you with us heart and soul? (*Crosses to table.*)

JASPER. (*coming to them*). Have no words! Just cut her throat.

VALDEZ. (*to* JASPER) No, I'll have no words with her. The American is growing uneasy. Let the girl go. I'll fix her after we get rid of the American.

JASPER. If you'll let me attend to him I'll warrant he won't be so impudent and bold.

VALDEZ. (*to* ELINORA) Some people might be offended at your silly remarks, but we are too sensible, and we don't notice it. Will you take a hand in the game we are about to play?

ELINORA. Not now. I will take a hand in the game you are going to play by and by.

VALDEZ. I don't quite catch your meaning.

ELINORA. I dare say you don't. However, we won't quarrel. Go and sit down. I'll make one of your merry party.

VALDEZ. (*to* LOPEZ) Lopez, we will adjourn to your private room. Every idiot has a right to this public apartment, it seems.

ELINORA. Make yourself at home, Mr. Idiot. Don't worry on my account. (*Goes up stage.*)

LOPEZ. You can retire to my room, señors.

PHELIM. This room is all right, and as for the kid yonder, she has a right to be in here. This is a public inn.

VALDEZ. You don't know whom to trust these times. Remember, the government has spies in all directions. I am not risking my head if you are.

PHELIM. I am an American citizen, and until I do something over here I defy Weyler, Spain, and the whole kitten crew of blackguards to lay a finger on me! That's what!

RICHARD. Señor Rial, if you choose to adjourn to another room, I am agreeable.

VALDEZ. I suggest this merely in the interest of safety.

RICHARD. Lead on, sir!

(*They arise and start to exit* R. 2 E. ELINORA *makes signals to* RICHARD *to attract his attention, but he fails to note them.*) PHELIM, *who is going out last, sees the motions and imitates them in a grotesque manner.*)

PHELIM. She thinks I belong to her lodge! She's giving me the grip and the password. " Erin go Bragh !"—" E Pluribus Onions !" " Cad Millia Failthey !" Ta-laa-loo-loo! (*Makes frantic and eccentric signals, and exits triumphant,* R. 2 E.)

ELINORA. He failed to note my signal of warning. He is lost if he remains here—what can I do? Return here as soon as possible, but not in this attire, for I believe the villain has partially penetrated this disguise. The maid engaged in this inn is in my pay; to her I will appeal for immediate aid. Come what may, the American must be saved!

(*Enter* CARL *at back.*)

CARL. Hello, you! Come here, I want to say something to you! Did you see two gentlemen fellers around here—one is a 'merican, the other a Micky Irishwoman?

ELINORA. I have no time, sir, to answer your questions. Seek the landlord in that room (*points* R. 2 E.) You will excuse me, I am in a great hurry. (*Exits,* L. I E.)

CARL. (*imitates voice*) Excuse me! I'm in a great hurry! Well, that lady isn't a bit obliging. Excuse me, I'm in a hurry! Get out, you Spanish cheroot! You ain't got any more sense than I've got. (BRIDGET *descends steps.*)

BRIDGET. Ah, ha! There you are! (*Grabs* CARL.) Now, my bucko, I have a hold on you! Where's that deceiving Irish friend of yours?

CARL. Cross my suspenders, I don't know where he is I'm looking for him, I tell you! You tell me where he is, and I'll tell you! What have I got to do with your troubles? Find him if you want him, but I ain't got nothing to do with your foolishness.

BRIDGET. Foolishness, is it? You'll find that I'm not fooling. He promised to marry me, and borrowed five dollars from me to buy the ring, and he lit out!

CARL. (*laughs*) He gave you de slip, did he?

BRIDGET. (*hits him*) What are you laughing at, you Dutch herring! I'll give you a smack that will knock you clean back to Germany like a sky-rocket!

CARL. My dear woman, I don't blame you for trying to find your mash, but don't soak me in the jaw like that.

BRIDGET. Well, I'll find him, so I will! And you'll go with me!

CARL. I'll go with you, " nit."

BRIDGET. You'll go with me nit is it? (*Slaps him.*) Nit is it?

CARL. I'll go with you nit, yes—I said mit you, not nit you! " Nit " means yes in German.

BRIDGET. (*crosses to* L.) I'll just keep my fins on you for safe keeping. Come right along, Mr. Smearcase; Ireland's got a hold of you now, and it's home rule or nothing.

CARL. This is tough on Germany! What's this world a coming to, when a woman can kidnap a man dis way and de poor sucker can't help himself! (*Business. She leads him out* L. I E. *He is protesting in vain.*)

(Enter ELINORA, *richly attired in* **Spanish** *female costume,*
door in flat.)

ELINORA. Perhaps I may be able to save him. I must
dissemble as much as possible. No harm must come to
Richard while I am here.

(Enter PHELIM, L. 1 E. *Begins a flirtation* **with her at** *once.)*

PHELIM. There's the Spanish beauty I met twice yester-
day—and I believe she's pretty well gone on me.
ELINORA. *(aside)* I must get rid of this troublesome ad-
mirer in some manner, and yet keep him near in case I
need his assistance.
PHELIM. *(comes to her)* You're a bird! I mean you're
pretty as a bird.
ELINORA. Ah, señor, you flatter me.
PHELIM. Not a bit of it. I bowed twice to you this afternoon. I'm a man that falls in love mighty quick!
ELINORA. The señor is a gallant man!

*(*PHELIM *has business of bowing.)*

PHELIM. Do you know that I think a great deal of you!
What is your name?
ELINORA. Helena Matanzas!
PHELIM. Is that so? What is it in English?
ELINORA. Same thing! Helena Matanzas.
PHELIM. You're one of the prettiest girls I've seen over
here. Now, then, I hate to be fooling around and wasting
time. I am one of these fellers that's quick! Now, what do
you? Will you marry me and become Mrs. Phelim McNab
instead of Helen Kansas?
ELINORA. Matanzas! .
PHELIM. Yes, Matanzas! Now, don't jump at me. I
know I'm a very fascinating man. I know you can't resist
me, but try to calm yourself and just show that you're anxious in a lady-like way.
ELINORA. Oh, señor, this is so sudden.
PHELIM. I told you I was a sudden man. Come, what
do you say about it?
ELINORA. *(aside)* I may as well carry out the joke just to
pacify him. *(Aloud)* Well, I'll tell you, we will have to
elope. You see, my uncle is a very peculiar man. He
watches me all the time. Disguised as my maid, we might
escape from here unobserved.
PHELIM. But where's my bustle, my dress, my other fixings to be a lady?

ELINORA.   I can get you some belonging to my maid.
I'll give you the signal by saying "molasses," and you are
to reply "taffy."

PHELIM.   I'll say molasses and you'll say taffy?

ELINORA.   No.   I say molasses.

PHELIM.   And I'm taffy.   But look here, you're not giving me taffy, are you?

ELINORA.   No; you'll get molasses.

(*Exits up steps.*)

PHELIM.   Oh, molasses, you sweet creature, you.   I feel
like a rainbow smothered in honey, wid a million angels
sprinkling gum drops over me.

(*Exit* L. 1 E.   *Introduce specialty.*)

ELINORA.   (*Entering, descends steps*)   At last I have a
moment to myself to watch over Richard Carson and warn
him of his great danger.   I have placed that warm-hearted
Irishman out of the way for the present, and I may be able
to pursue my way without interruption.

(*Enter* CARL, R. 1 E.)

CARL.   I got away from that Irish woman!   Ah!   There's
my idol!   Sweetest of Spanish womens, behold me at your
feet!   (*Kneels.*)   From the first time what I looked at you I
was struck!   I mean crazy foolish about you!   I never loved
anybody before, and this is my first offence!   I know that
that Irishman was making sheep's eyes on you, but he's no
good!   He buried seven wives in Ireland, and St. Patrick
chased him out for killing his grandfather!   Oh!   Miss—
Miss—what is your name?—I can't make resistance about
you!   If you don't have me I'll jump overboard and hang
myself!   I lay my Dutch heart at your feet and I accept
you!

ELINORA.   Rise!   (*He does so.*)   From the first time I saw
you I was struck with your manly beauty.

CARL.   Why, certainly!

ELINORA.   I could not be seen leaving this place with
you because my uncle and brothers watch every movement,
but, disguised as my maid, we could leave here with security.

CARL.   You want me to be a female womans?

ELINORA.   Yes.   I'll find garments for you.   Now, there
is no time for explanations.   I will throw a bundle out of
the window to you.   I will also attire myself differently to

avoid recognition. Now, go. I'll be waiting for you here
in the dark. To avoid mistakes I will say "molasses" and
you will say "taffy."

CARL. You put molasses on me and I give you taffy?

ELINORA. Remember what I said! Go—go—I hear
some one coming. My uncle must not see us together. Go
Don't stop to talk. (*She pushes him out* R. 1 E. CARL *attempts to talk.*)

CARL. But which do I say—syrup of figs or peanut
candy?

ELINORA. Go—go. We will be discovered. (*She forces
him out.*) At last! Was any one ever bothered in this way?
Well, I think it is the easiest way to rid myself of my ardent
admirers. Now, then, to discover Richard Carson's whereabouts, and leave my admirers to explain matters to each
other. I have something more serious to attend to than
love-making. (*Ascends stairs.*)

(*Enter* BRIDGET, R. 1 E.)

BRIDGET. The Dutchman gave me the slip. There's
some of the craziest lot of people around here I ever saw.
You can't get a civil answer nor information of any kind.

(CARL *enters* R. 1 E.)

CARL. What was that you said I'd say? You say molasses and I say taffy "tooty-frooty."

BRIDGET. What are you talking about?

CARL. I don't know; I'm in love.

(PHELIM *enters boldly from* L. 1 E., *but suddenly seeing*
BRIDGET *he darts under the table and hides.*)

BRIDGET. Where's Phelim McNab, I ask you?

CARL. Well, the last time I saw him— (PHELIM *hits*
CARL *on the foot with hand.*) Oh, the last time I seen him
I didn't saw him.

BRIDGET. Where did you see him?

CARL. Well, I saw him— (PHELIM *hits him.*) I didn't
see him until I looked at him. Nit, not, no.

BRIDGET. Of course you didn't, you idiot. Now answer
me, where was he and what was he doing? (PHELIM *hits*
CARL *again.*)

CARL. He was hitting me on de foot.

BRIDGET. What?

CARL. I say, he was standing on his feet.

(BRIDGET *steps on* PHELIM'S *hand unconsciously and keeps*

on talking to CARL. PHELIM *grimaces, squirms and groans, She's on my hand, she's standing on my fingers, etc.*)

BRIDGET.   You're a thick-headed fool. You know where Phelim is at this moment.   I wish I could stand on him.

PHELIM. (*aside*) You are standing on him.   Oh, she's like a ton of coal.

BRIDGET.   It won't be well for him when I lay my hands on him.   I've followed him over here, and you can bet your life I'll find him.   Bah! you Dutch fool, get away out of my sight!

CARL.   Yes, ma'am. (*She pushes him over; he scrambles to his feet; he loses his hat as he falls.* PHELIM *attempts to escape while her back is turned and drops his hat,* C., *and returns under table.* CARL *scrambles around near it and drops his hat. Picks up* PHELIM'S *and leaves his on the floor. Puts on* PHELIM'S *hat. Soon as* BRIDGET *sees it she screams.*)

BRIDGET.   The hat!   The hat!   It's Phelim's hat! (*Grabs it from* CARL'S *head, and shrieks in a hysterical manner.* PHELIM *escapes,* R. I E.)

CARL.   De woman is crazy!   Dat's my hat!

BRIDGET.   It's Phelim's hat—and he's here, or it's the ghost of his hat!   Where is he? (*Looks all around, and under table, still holding on to hat and* CARL.)   Come along, you'll help me to find him.   If he's in this house I'll have him, if I have to tear it down from roof to cellar!   Come along!   I've got his hat—and I'll find the rest of him—or I'll kill you!

CARL.   Here I go again!   I was going to get married, but now I'm going to get killed.   Oh, molasses! molasses! Save your own taffy! (*Begins to cry;* BRIDGET *drags him out,* R. I E. *Enter* VALDEZ, R. 2 E., *looks after* CARL *and* BRIDGET.)

VALDEZ.   There is no danger from that quarter, Our plot is progressing fairly well.   With that Irishman out of the way the end is near.   The American is engaged in a game of cards, and Lopez is watching an opportunity to drug his wine.

(*Enter* LOPEZ, R. 2 E.)

LOPEZ.   It's all right, Captain!   I had to wait my chance, but I gave him the drug all right.

VALDEZ.   Good!   Let him have another if you can get a chance—we'll make doubly sure.   He has got enough money to pay for any damage we may do to this old shanty.

LOPEZ. Where is that impudent girl?

VALDEZ. I don't know, and I'm not worried now, for you have succeeded. Let this room be kept dark for the present. (LOPEZ *takes the light.*) We will join the American, to avoid suspicion on his part.

LOPEZ. · What are you going to do with him?

VALDEZ. Don't ask silly questions. What would you do to a mad dog who threatened to bite you? (*Laughs and exits* R. 2 E. *with* LOPEZ.)

(*Enter* PHELIM R. I E., *disguised as "waiting maid;" female garments.*)

PHELIM. This is a nice get-up for a respectable man! How do women get along inside of these togs, I wonder? Well, I'm all ready to elope if my black-eyed charmer is ready and willing. It's dark enough and nobody will see us —I defy my own mother to know me.

(*Enter* CARL *in female garments,* L. 2 E.)

CARL. I'm a woman but I don't know it. I'm all ready for to slope off and get married to her. (*Sees* PHELIM.) Ah! There she is, Taffy Molasses!

PHELIM. Molasses taffy, butter scotch, and chewing gum.

CARL. Is that you, my darling?

PHELIM. Yes, Petty! I'm your own birdie, waiting to fly! (*They approach each other, and put arms around each other.*)

CARL. I was afraid you wouldn't keep your promises.

PHELIM. And I was afraid you'd throw me down! Ah, my darling, I love you so!

CARL. I love you harder than a dozen mules can kick. Give me one sweet kiss.

PHELIM. Certainly!—a dozen if you want them! I'm a bird at kissing! (*They prepare to kiss each other; they feel each other's faces; note the whiskers on chin or rough beard.*)

CARL. Your face is full of sand-paper and pimples.

PHELIM. And yours is like the rocky roads to Dublin.

CARL. Well, kiss me, sweetheart, and let us skip de gutter.

(*Just as they are about to kiss each other a noise is heard and* BRIDGET *comes down-stairs.* CARL *and* PHELIM *pick up their skirts and rush off* R. *and* L. BRIDGET *comes* C.)

BRIDGET. I thought I heard the sound of voices and

somebody scampering off. Well, I'm not surprised at any thing I see or hear in this crazy house.

(PHELIM *returns* L. 2 C.)

PHELIM. Molasses—taffy—molasses.

BRIDGET. Who the deuce is it that wants molasses?

PHELIM. There she is. (*Goes to* BRIDGET.) I thought I heard some one coming, that's why I scooted away. You're not angry with me, are you? (*Puts arms around her.*)

BRIDGET. What's going on here, I'd like to know.

PHELIM. We'll elope while we have the chance!

BRIDGET. It sounds like Phelim McNab's voice, or I'm a ghost! Is that you, Phelim?

PHELIM. Yes, Helene, your own Phelim is at your side. One sweet kiss and away we go! Fix your face and I'll give you a smack that would water a horse! (*He is just about to kiss her when* LOPEZ *enters* L. 1 E. *with a light.*) Holy Moses! It's Bridget!

BRIDGET. (*screams*) Phelim McNabs turned into a woman!

PHELIM. Legs, do your duty! (*Runs off, holding up skirts,* L. 1 E.)

BRIDGET. After him! Woman or no woman, I'll have every rag on him or her—whichever she or him happens to be.

(*Dashes off in pursuit. Soon as she exits* CARL *rushes in, bumps into* LOPEZ, *and both fall from the shock.* LOPEZ *throws candlestick after* CARL, *who scrambles to his feet and has funny business of escaping up-stairs—tripping over his female garments, falling down a few steps, and finally escaping up-stairs.* LOPEZ *groping to find candle, and with matches to relight candle during all of* CARL'S *ad lib. business of escaping up steps.*)

(*Enter* RICHARD, VALDEZ, JASPER, *and men from* R. 2 E.)

RICHARD. I believe I will bid you good-night. I feel very drowsy; a strange feeling seems to steal over me and my limbs refuse to bear me. (*Sinks in chair.*) What does this mean?

VALDEZ. It means, my fine American braggart, that you are drugged and in the power of Roderick Valdez.

RICHARD. Valdez! (*Attempts to rise.*) Coward!

VALDEZ. Yes, and you are helpless to defend yourself.

(*Laughs.*)   Look about you.   You are surrounded by men in my employ.   You will never leave this place alive!

RICHARD.   Would you murder me in my helpless condition?

VALDEZ.   I mean to burn down this place, and if you are able to crawl from the flames you are at liberty to do so. Bear him to the stairway and tie him. (JASPER *and men force* RICHARD *to stairs and bind him with rope. Soon as this is done* ELINORA *darts down stairs.*)

ELINORA.   Cowards!   Do you intend to murder this brave man?   Stand back!   You call yourselves men, but you are miserable dogs.

JASPER.   Out of the way, no power can save him now.

ELINORA.   I will save him or die by his side. (*Levels pistol at the group. They fall back.*)   Cowards! a woman is a match for such Spaniard curs as you are. (LOPEZ *steals behind her unobserved.*)

VALDEZ.   You are quite theatrical in your language and deeds, but you have reckoned without your host. (LOPEZ *suddenly seizes the pistol from her grasp and two men seize her quickly.*)   Now, my fair lady!   You see how easily the tables are turned when you are dealing with men of courage and intellect.

ELINORA.   Men of courage!   Vipers and crawling reptiles.   Men of courage do not war on women nor murder helpless men.

VALDEZ.   Look your last upon him!   Bear her into that room and lock the door. (*She is taken into* R. I E. *and door locked.*)   Now then apply the torch and let their cry for help be answered by the roaring flames. (LOPEZ *with a torch is seen to ignite the tow upon stairs, etc. Music. Flames appear* R. *and* L.   *Red fire under stairs.**)

VALDEZ.   Now then out of the building everybody.

(*All exit* R. I E.   ELINORA *batters down the door with an axe after crying for help in vain. She runs over to* RICHARD *and unties him and begins to assist him up the stairs just as* VALDEZ, JASPER, *and followers enter hurriedly,* L.)

VALDEZ.   By all the fiends, she has escaped from the room and is saving the American.   Shoot!   Shoot them down.   It's the Cuban spy!

**Arrange to make this an effective fire scene.*

(PHELIM *and* CARL *enter* L. U. E. *with guns, and level them at villains.*)

PHELIM.   Shoot if you dare !

CARL.   Down on your **knees** or I'll pepper you full **of** holes.   (*They cover* ELINORA'S *escape up the steps. Flames, smoke, etc.,* **add to the picture.** VALDEZ *and men are huddled down* L.)

CURTAIN

ACT III

SCENE.—*Old sugar house used as headquarters and prison by* VALDEZ (*see scene plot*). *Music.* JASPER *and several Spanish guerillas discovered in room,* L., *some seated on boxes.* JASPER *at small table, examining papers by aid of candle.*

JASPER. We've done much better than we expected. The Captain will be pleased with our work. It won't do to keep the prisoners in the other building—we'd better have them here where we can watch every movement.

(*Enter* SOPHIE, L., *a young Ingenue.*)

SOPHIE. Oh, Mr. Jasper, I wanted to tell you that the prisoners are quarreling, and one threatens to throw the other out of the window.

JASPER. I'll bet it's that Irishman. He'd try to quarrel with himself if he was the only one in the building.

SOPHIE. I think that's the very one that started the quarrel. He had the impudence to try to kiss me! He asked me if I'd miss a kiss, and I said that I wouldn't miss a kiss for anything, and he actually tried to kiss me then and there.

JASPER. Bring the prisoners into this building. (LOPEZ *exits* L.) They will be much safer, and leave room for quieter ones. (*To* SOPHIE.) You had better remain away from our American prisoners. They are too bold and impudent.

SOPHIE. Well, I rather like them to be smart and attentive! I don't like these drowsy kinds of men. Oh, if all Americans are like these prisoners, I'd like to get acquainted with them.

JASPER. The acquaintance won't last long—we'll soon be rid of them.

(LOPEZ *brings in* CARL *and* PHELIM *as prisoners, loaded down with chains, and seeming quite anxious to quarrel with each other.*)

PHELIM. I won't be hitched up with the Dutch! The idea of chaining me to that barrel of sour krout. It's an insult to Ireland, and I won't stand it.

32

CARL. Don't put airs on! Don't you think you're afraid of me! If you was twice as big as Ireland I wouldn't care! I don't want to be in company with you. Bite this chain in two, and you go my way and I'll go yours!

PHELIM. You'll not follow me around any more. Say you (*to* JASPER). Put this Dutchman into a jail by himself!

CARL. Yes—give me a bridle chamber all to my lonesome! Throw this in the cellar with the rats and the mices and the cockroaches.

PHELIM. If a rat would look at you it would have the jim-jams.

JASPER. Enough of this quarreling. Be pleasant to each other, for at daybreak you are to be shot!

PHELIM. Well, I'd rather be shot than have this Dutchman tagging around after me. (*Sees* SOPHIE.) Ah! there's the little beauty that brought my dinner to me! Ah! my, but she's sweet; and you're not married, are you?

SOPHIE. No, indeed; I'm still single.

PHELIM. Well, I don't blame you for being single. Look at the mugs of the men around you! They look like "Jo-Jo." Then look at me—a fine, handsome man! No wonder you're crazy about me. Can you blame her? Ah! if I wasn't chained up I'd make love to you and marry you in a minute!

SOPHIE. It's too bad you are all chained up! I feel sorry for you.

PHELIM. You're not half as sorry as I am!

JASPER (*to* LOPEZ). Place them in that room! (*Indicates room*, R.) See that everything is secure!

(LOPEZ *and a soldier attempt to put* PHELIM *and* CARL *into room*, R.)

PHELIM. Don't shove me. Don't put your dirty paws on me. Remember that President McKinley, Mark Hanna, and Jerry Simpson are looking at you! Don't shove me. I tell you— (*They are placed in room*, R., *and door in partition locked.*) Come in here, the whole lot of you, and I'll wipe the floor up with you. I can lick the whole Spanish army and old Weyler thrown in! You're afraid to come in here, you yaller-faced monkeys! Speaking of monkeys, there's a rat. (*Suddenly spies an imaginary rat off right. Seizes a stuffed club from floor and makes a dive to strike the rat. The sudden movement and lurch to* R. *pulls* CARL *down sprawling to the floor, and as they both sprawl on the floor they begin to pummel each other.* LOPEZ *opens the door, comes in to separate them. Both turn on* LOPEZ, *kick*

3

*and punch him until he dashes **out of room**, R., and hurriedly closes and locks the door.* CARL *and* PHELIM *shake hands and begin singing:)*

" Oh, the star-spangled banner in triumph shall wave
   O'er the land of the free and the home of the brave."

PHELIM. Let them come in again and interfere in our family matters again !
CARL. Germany and Ireland is united again ! Three cheers for me and myself!
PHELIM. No, no ; three cheers for me !
CARL. Three cheers for the both of us.
JASPER. *(to* LOPEZ) Don't bother with them. Let them remain there until the Captain disposes of them. *(Whistle heard off* L.) There is his signal Something of importance has occurred !

(Exit JASPER, LOPEZ, *and Soldiers* L. 3 E., *leaving* SOPHIE *alone in room,* L.)

PHELIM. I believe they've gone out! *(Peers through keyhole of door.)* There's no one in there but the girl. Now, Carl—don't let her look at your face, for you'll frighten her! I'm going to telephone to her. *(Through keyhole.)* I say, young woman—Miss—a—Miss—a—
SOPHIE. Sophie is my name !
PHELIM. Well, Sophia, come over here.
SOPHIE. I'm afraid to. If they catch me conversing with you there will be trouble.
PHELIM. A good smart, clever girl like you isn't going to be caught! Come over, my angel.
CARL. You could coax birds out of a tree! You're such a liar.

(SOPHIE comes to door.)

SOPHIE. What do you want ?   •
PHELIM. Are the rapscallions all gone ?
SOPHIE. They have gone into the other building.
PHELIM. Couldn't you open the door for a minute?
SOPHIE. No, indeed! The key is in the lock, but I wouldn't dare to touch it.
PHELIM. Ah ! you are a brave girl—beautiful and sweet as a hive full of honey! If I could only have another look at your sweet face I could die content. Just turn the key in the lock—that's a good girl.
CARL. Yes ; just twist it, twist it.

PHELIM. Shut up! There's no blarney in you! Your head is full of smearcase. (*To* SOPHIE) Go ahead, Sophie, dear—pretty little Sophie!

SOPHIE. I'm sure they'll be real angry if I open this door. There's a whole bunch of keys in the door.

PHELIM. I won't run away—we can't—we're chained hand and foot.

CARL. Yes; we're two pug dogs chained up.

PHELIM. Shut up, will you! (*To* SOPHIE) Sophie! if ever I get away from here, and I can induce you to go to the United States, I'll marry you. My father owns the United States mint, where they make all the money.

CARL. And my father owns a lot of pepper mint, where they make mint juleps!

SOPHIE. I'm so afraid I'll be caught by the soldiers. (*Unlocks door.*) There! I've unlocked the door, but you mustn't come out.

PHELIM. Why, of course not! Ah, Sophie, you're an angel. I'll buy you a pair of wings!

CARL. Yes; then you'll be "fly."

(PHELIM *comes out, dragging* CARL *with him.*)

PHELIM. How can I ever repay you, my darling Sophie, for your kindness (*embraces her*). There's a kiss for you. (CARL *tries to kiss her, but* PHELIM *prevents him.*) Not you. You're not in this. You don't belong to our lodge.

CARL. Well, I'm grateful, same as you are.

PHELIM. That may be, but you don't kiss Sophie. Sophie belongs to me. The idea of you trying to kiss Sophie! Why, it's obstropulous!

(JASPER *heard outside*, L.)

JASPER. Very well, Captain. It shall be attended to at once.

SOPHIE. Oh, they are returning! Quick, get into the room, so I can lock the door!

PHELIM. No; we'll lock the door. (*Takes bunch of keys.*) We'll lock ourselves in.

SOPHIE. Oh, no; that won't do.

PHELIM. Oh, yes, it will, Sophie darling. Sh— There's some one coming. Sneak out quick as you can. I'll meet you in here or outside. Go on, Sophie, if you love me! Be quick and skip!

SOPHIE. Oh, I don't know how this will end!

(*She exits*, L.)

PHELIM. I wish I did. Now then, Carl, try these keys and let's get the jewelry off of us. (*Tries keys.*) Ah, here's one! Hurroo! Erin go bragh! It's opened!

CARL. "De Wacht am Rhine! Kattufel salad and bumpernickel!" mine's off, too! (*They put chains into room,* R.)

PHELIM. Now then for liberty, and legs do your duty.

(*Just as they are about to exit,* L., BRIDGET'S *voice is heard off* L.)

BRIDGET. Will I ever find the right way out of here at all?

PHELIM. Murder in Irish, I'm in the soup! (*They start back toward partition as* BRIDGET *enters,* L. *She recognizes* PHELIM *and utters a cry of surprise.*)

BRIDGET. So I've got you at last, have I? What have you got to say for yourself?

PHELIM. (*to* CARL.) Get me out of this, and I'll never forget you.

CARL. (*aside to* PHELIM) Pretend that you're crazy; act natural. (*Crosses over to* BRIDGET) My dear woman, don't you see what's the matter?

BRIDGET. I see that I've got him, and he'll not get away from me, either.

CARL. Look at his eyes; look at that face; it looks like a slice of fried pie. Look at that mouth; it ain't got any express complexion about it. Don't you see what's the matter? De man is a lunaticle. He's crazy. (*To* PHELIM) Act like you was in de bug house—crazy, foolish.

BRIDGET. Phelim McNab crazy, is he?

CARL. He's got rats in his garret. Look at him. He's got soap suds coming out of his mouth. (PHELIM *begins a few violent contortions; twists his legs, grimaces and finally utters a yell.* BRIDGET *in alarm releases him and dodges behind* CARL *for protection.*)

CARL. Look him in the eye! Don't take your eyes off of him! He'll kill the whole two both of us.

PHELIM. You are my grandfather and you are my grandmother! I am a bicycle!

BRIDGET. He takes me for a velocipede and you for a wheelbarrow!

PHELIM. I'm a scorcher! Phew! See me going up a hill and down a hill! Is my lamp lit? Is my lamp lit?

CARL. He's turned into a lamp-post! Poor fellow! He don't know what I'm doing or what he did! He's crazy as a bedbug.

PHELIM. Hurrah! I've found a knife! (*Feels in pocket.*)

I'll kill you both and make you into rubber tires for my wheels! Your fat will make oil for my lamp and your bones will be spokes for my wheels! I'll paint the bike red with your blood!

CARL. I'll be darned if you do! You don't grease your bike with my oleomargarine!

BRIDGET. Hold him! Hold him!

CARL. Hold him yourself. I don't want him to bite me.

BRIDGET. Don't let him come near me! Are you a man?

CARL. Yes, but I'm not working at it. Do you take me for a fool to try to hold dot wild crazy Irishman? No, sir! I'm no loonitical asylum!

PHELIM. Stand where you are, both of you—the woman in particular. I'll have her life or I'll kill her!

BRIDGET. Bad luck to you, you'll not murder me if I know it! (*Short and wild chase ensues, and* PHELIM, *yelling like an Indian, chases them both off* L. 2 E.)

PHELIM. That's the way to get rid of her! The Dutchman's advice was good. She'll not bother me any more. (*Laughs.*) The crazy business is a great thing.

CARL. Well, Irish, I done it up in style for you, didn't I. Shake. (*They shake hands.*) Wasn't it a lucky thing I thought to make you crazy?

PHELIM. I haven't enjoyed myself so well since I had the "newmonia!" (*While they are thus laughing and complimenting each other* BRIDGET *enters at back from* L. *and comes down between them. They are laughing and hitting each other on the back. Suddenly* CARL *looks up and sees her. He droops and falls with astonishment.* PHELIM *then sees her, and begins a wild series of contortions to impress her with his "crazy antics."*

BRIDGET. You can't work that on me. I'm on to your tricks. You're crazy, are you? And this Dutchman wants to make a fool of me, does he? I'll bring you to your senses, so I will. (*Beats* CARL *with umbrella. He runs off* L. 2 E. PHELIM *tries to dodge her, but she seizes him by the coat. He slips out of his coat and escapes* L. 2 E.) You'll not get away from me again. (*Sees coat.*) Well! He's skinned out of his coat like an eel. Stop him! Stop the crazy man! (*Chases off after* PHELIM, *waving the coat.*)

(LOPEZ *enters* L.)

LOPEZ. There's that wild Irishwoman again. She seems to be everywhere we go. (*Goes over to partition.*) Hello! The door is opened (*looks in*) and the prisoners gone!

Here's a nice fix. If the Captain finds it out I'll be shot instead of them. (*Finds keys.*) I'll just lock the door and keep mum about it. Oh, these Americans! these Americans! Now you've got 'em and now you haven't got 'em!

(*Enter* VALDEZ, L. JASPER *and men follow in, having* RICHARD *bound and a prisoner.*)

VALDEZ. For the short time you have to remain on earth this will be your place of safe keeping, and I assure you that the Cuban spy will not lend a helping hand to your escape. Make your peace with heaven, for your time is short.

RICHARD. Fool that I was not to see through your disguise and clumsy plot to entrap me.

VALDEZ. You will admit that you Americans are not as smart as you give yourselves credit to be.

RICHARD. In treachery and low cunning you excel any other race of people. Is it manly to drug a man and then leave him to perish in the flames? Is this the boasted courage of Weyler's representative?

VALDEZ. Fume and fret as much as you like. I laid the trap for you and you stepped into it. Your friend the Cuban spy has brought you to a nice pass.

RICHARD. You pretended to be a friend of the patriots while in the States. You are doubly a scoundrel for such pretensions. You persecute a woman and you are a cur and a coward for doing so.

VALDEZ. That woman is in my way and I have ample reasons for her removal. As to the patriots, misguided wretches, one and all, they'll either hang or be shot down soon as captured.

RICHARD. That is your mode of warfare, is it? Guerrillas, robbers, cut-throats!

VALDEZ. We conduct our warfare to suit ourselves, and we will not ask the American government for its advice on that matter. If you are a citizen of that boastful nation, what are you doing over here?

RICHARD. Aiding by my voice and means the independence of Cuba! Joining the struggling men who are seeking to free themselves from the hated rule of Spain and such wretches as yourself and the craven Weyler!

VALDEZ. Put a bridle upon your tongue!

RICHARD. I have not yet been taken with arms in my possession, nor in an act of hostility. I have a right as a man to express my opinion, and I shall continue to do so.

VALDEZ. You have been captured, you'll admit.

RICHARD. By treachery, as the brave Maceo was taken and murdered. But there is a day of retribution for such as you and your master in Havana!

VALDEZ. Think of your own fate. Your life hangs by a single thread. Lopez, did you remove the prisoners in that room to place this one in it?

LOPEZ. (*hesitates*) No—yes—I mean—the room is empty, as you ordered!

VALDEZ. Conduct the American into it. See that the ropes are tight and secure. When next you emerge from that room it will be for your execution.

RICHARD. I defy you!

VALDEZ. Will you tell me where to find that girl—the spy?

RICHARD. No; I would rather die than speak a single word that would place her in the power of such a villain as you are. (*Exit* RICHARD.)

(*Music.* ELINORA *attired as a Sister of Charity or " Red Cross" Society.*)

ELINORA. I came to offer consolation to those condemned and about to die.

VALDEZ. They do not need it, nor would they accept it, I am sure.

ELINORA. All men need consolation in their last hours. No matter how wicked, there is still a desire to repent on the part of all who have led evil lives when death is at hand.

VALDEZ. These Americans seem to care for nothing! While I do not wish to prevent you in your work of mercy, you will find it fruitless and barren of good results.

ELINORA. I am sure of good results, if the prisoner will but listen to my words of consolation.

VALDEZ. But he is a heartless villain!

ELINORA. Let him who is without sin cast the first stone! Would you see him die unprepared?

VALDEZ. It matters not to me. I obey my military rules and my commanding officer.

ELINORA. Has General Weyler condemned this American so soon to death?

VALDEZ. I am commanding this detachment of Spanish volunteers. This man is a spy, and he has been captured with important documents in his possession.

ELINORA. Are you speaking the truth?

VALDEZ. I am! But visit the prisoner if you will. His

time is short, therefore you have but a few moments to
ease his conscience.

ELINORA.   A few moments will be sufficient!

VALDEZ.   Lopez, admit her to the room! (LOPEZ *opens
door*—ELINORA *slowly enters*.) Lopez—hearken to every
word uttered! (LOPEZ *listens at half-open door*).

ELINORA (*to* RICHARD). I came to offer words of consolation! You are soon to die, and innocent or guilty you
should be prepared. (RICHARD *looks up, and recognizes
her*.)

RICHARD.   Elinora!

ELINORA.   Richard! You here! (*Makes a warning
motion to lip, and speaks low*) 'Sh! We are observed, and
every word listened to! (*louder*) Think of your fate, and
be prepared to meet it.

RICHARD.   I am! I came to Cuba to aid in a glorious
cause. I am in the hands of the merciless guerillas, but I
will die an American, breathing defiance to the end, and
shouting "Cuba Libre!"

ELINORA.   We should forgive our enemies.   Here!
(*lower*) I place this pistol within your breast. Make good
use of it should needs be. (*As she speaks, she places a
revolver within his vest*) Do not despair! I will never
desert you! (*rises*) Farewell! Meet your fate as becomes
a brave man, and trust to One above who hearkens to those
in affliction—He who rewards the innocent and punishes
the guilty. (*Passes out of room*—LOPEZ *locks the door*.)
The prisoner is prepared. I have succeeded in obtaining
good results.

VALDEZ.   I am pleased to think you have succeeded!

ELINORA.   Considering the surroundings, better than I
expected.

VALDEZ.   I may require your kind services soon.   I
need consolation at times.

ELINORA.   When that time arrives, rest assured I will be
present, I hope. (*Exits*, L.)

VALDEZ. (*to* LOPEZ) Follow her, see where she goes, and
report everything to me. I half distrust her. And Lopez,
let me warn you about drinking—keep your head clear.
There is important work ahead for us.

LOPEZ.   I'm not drinking, sir!

VALDEZ.   I warn you to remain sober. Follow that
person, and be quick about it. (LOPEZ *exits*, L. *He has
been showing signs of liquor since he entered*) Jasper, I
think we had best avoid further delay.

JASPER.   In which way?

VALDEZ. This American has crossed me several times, and the sooner we dispose of him the better. His government will never make inquiries after him, and furthermore, he is here in arms against us.

JASPER. He has not been captured in open warfare nor has he as yet committed any act against our government.

VBLDEZ. Very true. But what does that matter? We have Americans and Cubans in jail for doing much less, and who is to prevent us from putting them out of the way if we condemn them?

JASPER. That's very true. This American has interfered in your personal matters and you now have the power to remove him.

VALDEZ. Yes, and I'll do it. Jasper, you don't know the danger surrounding me while that Cuban spy lives. So far she has not identified me, and I do not propose to give her the opportunity. Do you see this? (*Shows mark in palm of hand.*)

JASPER. A brand! A brand that could be recognized anywhere.

VALDEZ. So far she has not seen it, and I'll take precious good care that she won't. (*Enter* LOPEZ, L.) Well, what did you discover?

LOPEZ. Nothing. She went into the other building and then I lost track of her altogether.

VALDEZ. You addle-headed fool! I told you to follow close upon her track. You've been drinking again.

LOPEZ. 'Pon my word, Captain, I'm sober as a judge.

VALDEZ. Watch the building and bring me all the information possible. Go. (LOPEZ *exits*, L., *partially staggering.*) It won't do to trust that fellow with any important mission. He's growing worse and worse. Now about this American. I have decided to rid myself of him at once.

JASPER. We are here to obey!

(*Enter* SOPHIE, L.)

SOPHIE. Captain, did you know that one of the prisoners has escaped.

JASPER. Escaped! Which one?

SOPHIE. (*hesitates*) The fat one—the German. I saw him running away like a race horse. He's the only one I saw. I didn't see the other one, the real nice one—indeed I didn't. I didn't see him at all. (*Begins to cry.*) I don't know where he is. I didn't see him.

VALDEZ. No one has accused you of complicity. You

saw one of them running away, did you? Which way did
he go—over the right?

SOPHIE.   No ; over the left.

VALDEZ.   Give the alarm at once.   He may be recap-
tured.

(JASPER *exits with men*, L.)

SOPHIE. I'm so glad they won't catch the Irishman! Oh,
but he's cunning, and he knows just how to kiss a girl!
(*Exits*, L.)

(*Enter* JASPER *and guerillas having* ELINORA *in charge.
They bring her* C. *Sentinel at door with Cuban boy.*)

JASPER.   Captain, you are in rare luck.   Look.   Do you
recognize this person?   We found her close to this building.

VALDEZ. (*gazes at her*) The Cuban spy!

ELINORA.   Yes, the Cuban spy!   But it took a dozen of
your "brave" men to bring Little Cuba to their brave com-
mander.

VALDEZ. So you are masquerading in the costume of the
Cuban rebels.

ELINORA.   Not Cuban rebels—Cuban patriots ; men striv-
ing to gain independence for their country.   I am not masquerading, as you are; I am just what you see me.   I am
not a hypocrite, pretending to aid a cause and willfully betraying my fellow-men to the merciless Spaniard.

RICHARD. Elinora is in their hands!   Why did she venture here again?

VALDEZ.   You possess valuable information concerning
the insurgents.   What is their strength?   Where are they
at present?   Give me a list of their leaders and you are
free to go.

ELINORA.   Not if you were to doom me to a death of
tortures.   I am a Cuban, and I never betray my com-
panions.

VALDEZ. But it means life to you.

ELINORA. I will never purchase life with dishonor. You
may kill me if you will, but you cannot force me to speak.

VALDEZ. (*crosses to* C.) Were you not a woman I would
strike you to my feet.

ELINORA.   And if you were a man you wouldn't threaten
a woman.

VALDEZ.   Don't tempt me too far or I'll forget that you
are a woman.

ELINORA.   That would be nothing new to you.   You

sought my life on the blockade runner and encouraged
your ruffianly crew to destroy me.

VALDEZ. Silence, or (*produces pistol*) I'll end your
career.

ELINORA. I see that, and I go you one better. (*Levels
revolvers at* VALDEZ.) Brave men! (*Laughs.*) You shrink
from a woman. The first one who makes a movement
toward his belt dies upon the spot. Place that weapon
upon the floor! (VALDEZ *does so.*) And you (*to* JASPER)
follow suit. (*She compels them to place weapons upon the
floor. Soon as all have laid arms upon the floor,* PHELIM,
attired as counterpart of LOPEZ, *staggers in* L. *He makes
his way toward* ELINORA, *and behind her as she is commanding the guerillas to lay down their arms. Soon as* VALDEZ
sees LOPEZ *he becomes reassured.*)

VALDEZ. Seize her, Lopez, quick! Disarm her!

PHELIM. I'm not Lopez, but Phelim McNab, at your service. (*Throws off hat and shows features.*) I'm with the
Cuban spy. (*Levels pistol at them.*)

VALDEZ. Tricked again! and by these Americans!

PHELIM. Make way there, you yaller-faced gorrillas.
Pick up the artillery, Elinora! (*She picks up weapons.*) Now,
then, retreat in good order, with your face to the foe!

ELINORA. And if harm comes to the American prisoner
we'll burn down this building and every Spaniard in it.
Phelim! away for our friends while I hold these brave men
at bay!

PHELIM. Don't take your eyes off of them. Pop them
over if they look cross-eyed! We can lick a million of
consumptive monkeys like this. Oh, but you're a pudding
for us. (*Exits* L.)

ELINORA. I will be at this door; make but a single hos-
tile movement and I'll fire. The Cuban band of patriots
are close at hand. Harm Richard Carson at your peril! the
Cuban spy is still your master! (*She exits* L., *covering* VAL-
DEZ *and his followers with her revolvers as she exits backing
off; then she closes the door,* L.)

VALDEZ. Why do you all stand petrified! Are you all
afraid of a woman?

JASPER. Captain, you didn't appear to be any too anxious to face those revolvers yourself. The girl is desperate
and she meant business.

VALDEZ. She has taken our arms and she says the rebels
are close by.

JASPER. Our arms are not all gone! (LITTLE CUBA *is
seen at grated window in* RICHARD'S *room.*)

VALDEZ. Not all gone? Where have you enough to arm your men?

JASPER. In the prisoners' room! There are rifles loaded and ready for use.

VALDEZ. Loaded and ready for use?

JASPER. I loaded them myself.

(*By this time* ELINORA *has entered* RICHARD'S *room. She motions him to be quiet, and searching in a corner sees the rifles stacked behind some bags and boxes* L. U. *corner.*)

VALDEZ. Then I will put them into immediate use.

JASPER. To repel the attack?

VALDEZ. No—to shoot that American dog. That will be one less standing in my way.

(*During this conversation* ELINORA *is seen to remove the cartridges from the rifles and cast them away.*)

JASPER. Then the quicker you carry out your threat the better.

(*Soon as possible* ELINORA *unties* RICHARD'S *arms. She has barely time to do this when* JASPER *is at the door unlocking it.*)

ELINORA. (*to* RICHARD) Fear not—friends are near you. (*She hides behind bags up stage; the door is opened by* JASPER.)

VALDEZ. Take those rifles and shoot down the American.

(*Rifles are passed out by* JASPER *to men who aim at* RICHARD *as they stand at open door.*)

VALDEZ. The Cuban spy vowed to save you! Let her do so now, my bold American. (*To men*) Take good aim —Fire!

(*Music. Guns miss fire.* RICHARD *instantly shows that his hands are free, and he produces a pistol from bosom.* ELINORA *jumps out from hiding place with brace of revolvers leveled at* VALDEZ *and men.*)

ELINORA. Surrender, in the name of the Republic of Cuba and the United States of America.

(PHELIM *and* CARL, *with guns, appear from* L., *thus hemming in the Spaniards and placing them between two fires.* PHELIM *and* CARL *dancing with joy.* ELINORA *and* RICHARD *in room,* R., *keeping ruffians in* C.)

CURTAIN

ACT IV

SCENE.—*Handsome parlor. Hotel at Pinar del Rio. See scene plot.*

(*Music. Enter* RICHARD; *evening dress.*)

RICHARD. The American Minister is to call and receive a delegation of American citizens here in Cuba, to investigate the outrages. A reception is to be given in his honor, and I dare say that for the present our troubles are over.

(*Enter* CARL, *door* C., *extravagant missfit suit.*)

CARL. Ah! Mr. Carson, we're right in it now. When they see me they'll drop dead. I hunted all over this place for a nice suit, and I got it.

RICHARD. You look very well, indeed.

(PHELIM *heard outside.*)

PHELIM. You needn't bother yourself; I'll find the parlor. This isn't the first time I've been in a hotel, by a "darn site." (*Enters door*, C., *eccentric full dress.*) Hello, fellers! How's my togs? I don't feel at home in these dude fixings. It's like being in a straight jacket. What's going on here to-night? (*Sees* CARL) Ah! get on to the bag of oats! Now you do look like a bologna sausage.

CARL. Well, I don't look like a whiskey barrel, anyway.

PHELIM. Indeed you don't, for if you did I'd tap you in a minute. But tell us, Mr. Carson, where's the General?

RICHARD. The General?

PHELIM. Yes, the General! Elinora, the Cuban spy. The one that got us out of all the scrapes!

RICHARD. She'll be here in a moment.

PHELIM. I hope she's not flirting with any of those Spanish galoots.

RICHARD. At present the Spaniards are far from this town. This place is in the hands of a few patriot Cubans. After defeating Valdez and placing him in the hands of the Cubans, we came here to take part in the American minister's investigations. He is expected here shortly.

PHELIM. I don't care for him! I want to see "our" General. I've gone to a lot of trouble to get fixed up to dazzle her, and I'm here to dazzle.

RICHARD. You shall be gratified, for here she is.

45

(*Music.* ELINORA *enters in evening costume, door,* C. *Comedians have business of extravagant bowing* R. *and* L., *kicking up their heels.*)

PHELIM.   My, oh, my! But ain't she pretty as a humming-bird!

CARL.   She's beautiful as my picture!

PHELIM.   Shut up! What do you know about beauty, anyway?

ELINORA.   Gentlemen, I am pleased to see you, but wish to say this: Do not fancy that we rest here in security, for scouts have been coming in and going out of the city all the afternoon. It may be that Weyler's men have approached the city.

PHELIM.   That's all right. I can fight in these togs just as well as I can in my working clothes.

CARL.   Yes: I don't care if I get shot all dressed up!

RICHARD.   With your permission I will go at once and investigate. Come, Carl—I may need you! Elinora! You will kindly excuse me! (*Exits, door,* C.)

CARL.   You will kindly excuse myself! (*Bows and exits.*)

PHELIM.   The dude clothes will drive that Dutchman crazy! (*sits in chair*) My, but I can't keep my eyes off of you—you look so pretty!

(*Enter* VALDEZ, R. I E. *He pauses as he recognizes* ELINORA.)

VALDEZ.   So—we meet again, but the meeting is not quite unexpected!

ELINORA.   Why are you here?

VALDEZ.   To appear before the American minister and refute the fabrications that will be told him.

ELINORA.   You are very bold to venture here. Are you aware that I can deliver you into the hands of General Maximo Gomez?

VALDEZ.   Indeed! And if you do so you will be kind enough to say that you found me in the regular service of the Spanish government.

ELINORA.   I will do nothing of the kind. You made war upon the poor Cubans as pirates upon the high seas. You lack the manhood to enlist in the Spanish regulars. You prefer to be a robber, a villain, and to fight as savages. You must take the consequences.

VALDEZ.   But who can prove that I was not an enlisted man?

ELINORA.   I can! I know you, Roderigo Valdez. I

know you thoroughly. When Richard Carson was in your power you made ready to shoot him down like a dog. When you discovered me upon the blockade runner you sought my life. You have never spared any one who fell into your hands. You are a traitor to the cause of Cuba. You have betrayed every leader of our struggling army. You showed no mercy. So expect none in return.

PHELIM. Hurrah! That's the kind of talk. When St. Patrick drove all the snakes out of Ireland some of them got over here, and I'll bet that his great grandfather was an anaconda or a sea serpent, or the daddy of all the snakes.

VALDEZ. Very well. I am forearmed.

ELINORA. Phelim, mount the horse which is saddled and ready in the court-yard. Take this message to General Gomez. (*Gives paper to* PHELIM. CARL *appears at door.*)

PHELIM. But I never rode a horse in all my life. Let the Dutchman go.

CARL. Oh, no! You don't catch me on the back of a horse.

PHELIM. All right. I'll chance it. Keep your eye on that villain, CARL. Good-bye Helen Matanzas. Your molasses obeys you. (*Exits* C. D.)

CARL. Is that Irishman going to ride a horse? Good-bye, Irishman. (*Stands at window and speaks.*) There he goes. He's climbing on the horse's back. Now he's trying to hold on. Now the horse is trying to stand on his head. Now the horse is dancing a jig—and—and now they're off. (*Horse imitation of clattering hoofs and they die away.*)

VALDEZ. (*aside*) She has sent a message to Gomez. If it reaches him and I am taken, all is lost. I must warn my followers. (*Aloud*) I leave you to your excellent friend. I assure you that we will meet again shortly.

(*Exits* R. 1 E., *bowing coldly.*)

CARL. Go to the donner und blitzen!

ELINORA. Carl, follow that man! See where he goes and whom he meets. Don't lose track of him.

CARL. I'll stick to him like a porous plister.

(*Exits* R. 1 E.)

ELINORA. I must warn Richard at once. Valdez is here for mischief.

(*Exits* L. 1 E. *Enter* BRIDGET, C. D.)

BRIDGET. Well, it seems that the more I learn the less I

know. And the further I walk the more I travel. I've been
on the track of Phelim McNab and caught him, and when
I'd catch him I wouldn't have him. I never saw such a lot
of contradictions in all my life, and here I am trying to catch
a runaway lover that as soon as I catch him I haven't got
him. I'll leave Cuba, for I'm disgusted with everything and
everybody!

(Enter RICHARD, D. C.)

RICHARD. I must confess that I am in the toils of Cupid
at last. Elinora has been far more dangerous than the bul-
lets of the Spaniards, for her eyes have reached my heart
and made me a willing prisoner.

(BRIDGET *comes down behind him and suddenly throws her
arms around him.)*

BRIDGET. Oh, Captain dear! You're just the very one to
aid a poor, distressed woman whose heart is breaking, and
all on account of love!

RICHARD. Yes, my good woman, I'm willing to aid you,
but not quite so willing to accept this demonstration of affec-
tion. *(Attempts to release himself.)*

BRIDGET. Any port in a storm! My heart needs consolation, and I can't bear to be alone in my grief.

(ELINORA *enters,* L.)

ELINORA. Ah, ha! My fickle Captain, I have caught you,
have I? Keep right on. Don't mind me. Don't let me put
a stop to your love-making. *(Aside)* I'd like to scratch her
eyes out.

RICHARD. But I assure you that I am not in the act of
love-making. Please don't go. *(To* BRIDGET) Remove your
arms. What do you mean?

BRIDGET. I want somebody to protect me, and you're
just the one! (RICHARD *removes her arms.)*

ELINORA. I did not know that you could find time for
love-making while surrounded by our enemies. But pray,
don't stop on my account. I wouldn't for the world interfere between sweethearts! It was so mean of me to come
in so abruptly—but I couldn't help it.

RICHARD. Why will you misunderstand everything and
tantalize me in this manner?

ELINORA. You seem to enjoy the misunderstanding very
much, and I'm sure it is not very tantalizing to have a lady's
arms about your neck, is it? *(Laughs.)* Ah! Americans are
such peculiar people.

BRIDGET. I came over to Cuba to find a husband, and I won't go back without one.

ELINORA. The Captain will make a most lovable one, I'm sure. But go on—arrange for the wedding—and the honeymoon. I wish you joy, Mr. Carson !

RICHARD. Enough of this nonsense! (*To* BRIDGET) Go and seek your promised husband and do not annoy me again. (*Crosses*, R.)

BRIDGET. Oh, very well! There's just as good fish in the sea as ever was caught—but I'm not going to spend all my days a fishing! Farewell to you. I'll find my Phelim McNab without the help of either one of you! You're jealous of my good looks ; and the next time I look for consolation I'll not come to you. If you see Mr. McNab, "Just tell him that you saw me." (*Exits* C. D.)

ELINORA. By the way, do you know that danger threatens.

RICHARD. Perhaps it is an idle rumor. So far I have heard nothing to alarm us.

ELINORA. This is no time for surmises. I have sent a message to General Gomez for help ; meanwhile the prisoners must be looked after. Valdez is a most dangerous man, either as a captive or at liberty.

RICHARD. Not half as dangerous as you are.

ELINORA. Or Bridget Monahan! I dare say you are lonesome, now that she is gone and your love-making is at an end. (*Crosses to sofa*, R.)

RICHARD. Please be serious for a moment. We are in danger until we reach the patriot camp. I ask the privilege of remaining with you to protect you—if need be, to die for you.

ELINORA. Extends, then, your devotion so far?

RICHARD. It is a man's duty to protect a woman—at all places—under all circumstances.

ELINORA. Is there no other reason?

RICHARD. Do you wish me to be perfectly frank with you?

ELINORA. Does not the danger which surrounds us warrant naught but candor?

RICHARD. Then it will be a pleasure to defend you—for, Elinora, I love you. (*Crosses to* L.)

ELINORA. You love me? You know nothing concerning me. You know me only as Elinora—one who pursues a villain to avenge a father's murder. You know me as the Cuban spy—a waif—a spy in the cause of Cuba to further my plans and to aid my country. Yet you tell me that you love me?

4

RICHARD.   I do.   You are dearer to me than life.   (*Puts arm about her.*)

ELINORA.   When retribution has overtaken my father's destroyer, I will say, Richard Carson, I love you!

(*Enter* BRIDGET *at back*, L.)

BRIDGET.   Ah, ha!   What do I see?   Oh, don't stop on my account.   I wouldn't for the world interfere between sweethearts.   It was mean of me to bounce in here so disreputably, but I couldn't help it.   Arrange for the wedding and the honeymoon.   Americans are such peculiar people. (RICHARD *and* ELINORA *exit*, L., *laughing*.)   Everybody is going daffy around here.   There's another poor man gone! Oh, my! oh, my! what poor luck I have with the men.   I wish I could find a rabbit's foot for luck!   (*Exits*, L.)

(*Enter* PHELIM *at back*.)

PHELIM.   I succeeded all right.   I met one of the General's men coming towards this stockade, and I gave him the message, and I walked back.   I wouldn't ride on that horse's back for a fortune.   I'm not a circus rider, by any means.

(*Enter* SOPHIE, R. I E.)

SOPHIE.   Ah, there you are!   (*Runs to him.*) I've been looking for you everywhere since you left the old sugarhouse.   (*Puts arm around him.*) I was so lonesome that I had to start out to find you.   You don't seem glad to see me.

PHELIM.   Oh, yes, I am.   I'm as glad as if I'd lost a leg.

SOPHIE.   And I came so far to see you'

PHELIM.   Of course you have, and I was just going to start on a trip to see you.   (*Enter* BRIDGET *at back*, L. *Stands horrified at seeing them*) And I was about to say— (*Discovers* BRIDGET) Oh! Holy Moses and blue blazes!

SOPHIE.   Where?

PHELIM. (L. C., *points toward* BRIDGET.   SOPHIE *screams and faints in his arms*.   BRIDGET *comes down* C.)

BRIDGET.   Who's that woman you're holding in your arms?

PHELIM.   Which arms?   Which woman?

BRIDGET.   That woman there!

PHELIM.   (*points to* SOPHIE) Oh, this!   You mean this woman here?   Well, well—this woman here?

BRIDGET.   Yes, I mean that woman there.   How came she there?

PHELIM. Yes; how came she there! This woman came here, and that's how she got there—and there she is, and here she is.

BRIDGET. Who is she? I've asked you!

PHELIM. Who is she? Oh! you want to know who she is. Oh! she's a she—can't you see she's a woman?

BRIDGET. I ask you for the last time, Who is that woman in your arms?

PHELIM. (aside to SOPHIE) It's a crazy woman—we'll have to humor her. (Aloud) This woman, madam, is—is— my sister Sadie.

SOPHIE. Not Sadie—Sophie.

PHELIM. Yes—Sophie—Sadie!

BRIDGET. Your sister! You never told me you had a sister.

PHELIM. Well, I didn't know it myself. You see I was away from home when it happened!

BRIDGET. So this is your sister?

PHELIM. Yes—my own dear sister Stella!

BRIDGET. Stella! You said her name was Sophie Sadie!

PHELIM. So it is—Sophie Sadie Stella. She can have as many names as she likes. It's none of my business.

BRIDGET. Well, how old is your sister?

PHELIM. She's older than me—I mean I'm younger than she is, of course. You see I'm twenty-four, and Sarah is twenty-one.

BRIDGET. Sarah! I thought you said her name was Sophie Sadie Stella?

PHELIM. So it is—Sophie Sadie Stella Sarah! Oh, she's got names to burn! She's got lots of names—and that's all she's got. Now, you see, when Susan was born—

BRIDGET. Susan! Susan! Is her name Susan now?

PHELIM. No—not Susan Now—Susan McNab—Sophie Sadie Stella Sarah Susan—now do you see?

BRIDGET. Yes, I see.

PHELIM. Well, that's more than I do!

SOPHIE. Who is this woman!

PHELIM. (aside to SOPHIE) Hush! A crazy woman! She has an idea that I'm in love with her. We'll keep it up!

BRIDGET. What are you whispering about?

PHELIM. Whispering here to Salantha!

BRIDGET. Salantha! You just said her name was a whole lot of names and Susan!

PHELIM. Of course I did—but we call her Salantha for short. Salantha is the Irish for Susan,

BRIDGET. Where was Salantha born?

PHELIM.   At home, of course!

BRIDGET.   I mean where, and when?

PHELIM.   Ask her yourself—she was present at the time
I wasn't.

BRIDGET.   Was she born in Ireland, or wasn't she?

PHELIM.   I think she was born away from Ireland—I'm
not sure.   You see I was over in America at the time, and
I got a telegraph, saying—" you've got a sister, and it's a
female !"

BRIDGET.   I think you're telling me a lie, and I'll find out
for myself.   Stand out of my way, and I'll investigate this!

PHELIM.   Go ahead! Investigations never amount to
anything.

BRIDGET.   Well, I'll make this amount to something or
I'll break every bone in your body.

(BRIDGET *goes over to* SOPHIE *in a very threatening manner.*)

PHELIM.   Now, ladies, don't fight over me as if I was a
bone or a mouse.

BRIDGET.   I want to know by what right you allow this
man to put his arms around you.   He's not your brother,
and you're not his sister.

SOPHIE.   And by what right do you question me about
this handsome man?

BRIDGET.   Because he promised to marry me.

SOPHIE.   He promised the same thing to me.

BRIDGET.   Oh, the bigamist—the trigamist! I'll settle it
right here.

PHELIM.   Settle it among yourselves.   I've got a divorce
from you both.   (*He rushes up stage and escapes* C. D.   *Both
women chasing after him and shouting,* " *Stop him !* " " *Head
him off !* " " *Stop him !* " " *Stop our husband !* " *etc., and amid
much bustle exit after him, pushing each other out of the way
to overtake* PHELIM *and get him first.*)

(CARL *enters,* R. I E.)

CARL.   I guess that feller won't make us any trouble.
He is sitting on the piazza smoking a cigaroot.   I've got
somebody watching him, all right.

(*Enter* ELINORA, R.)

ELINORA. (L. C.) Is that you, Carl?

CARL.   Oh, she calls me Carl.   Lie still, my pilpertating
heart, lie still.   (*Aloud*) Yes, it is your own Carl—your
Carlo.   Oh, Helen Matanzas, molasses taffy, now is my

chance to declaration my love to you. Have pity on a love-sick Dutchman. This is my first offense. I'm green in the business. Don't fall in love with that Irishman. The Irish want everything they see in this world.

ELINORA. Arise! I promise you that I will not enter-tain the Irishman's proposals of marriage. (*Crosses to* L.)

CARL. Well, if I'm going to be the happy man, why, molasses, give taffy just one little kiss.

ELINORA. Blindfold yourself, Carl; that's the only way I'll consent.

CARL. All right; make me blindfolded. (*She blindfolds* CARL *with kerchief.*)

ELINORA. Now then, Carl, earn your kiss.

(*She eludes him and exits laughing,* L. 1 E. *As he is groping about* BRIDGET *enters* L. U. E. *She is seized by* CARL.)

CARL. Now I've got you, molasses, and I want a dozen kisses. (*Begins to kiss her; tears off kerchief, sees his mistake, utters a yell of surprise and dashes off,* C. D., *pur-sued by* BRIDGET, *shouting "Give me the dozen."*)

(*Enter* PHELIM, L. 1 E.)

PHELIM. It's worth a man's life to be around loose in this part of the country. The women are crazy, I believe. If I had my way they'd all be put behind locks and bars to keep them quiet. I imagine I see a woman behind every bush or tree with a net to catch me. Bridget's the most persistent woman I ever saw.

(*Enter* CARL, *running,* C. D., *and bumps into* PHELIM.)

CARL. Oh, it's you, is it? I thought it was that Irish-woman! She's here again.

PHELIM. I know she's here. I've just slid out of her hands like an eel.

CARL. By jiminy, so did I! But here she comes on the double quick.

PHELIM. So she is. What's to be done? Get me out of this scrape and I'll never forget you.

CARL. Lay down quick and pretend that you're dead.

PHELIM. First you have me crazy, now you want me dead.

CARL. If you don't die now she'll catch you, and you'll be dead for a long time. Quick! Die—die! (PHELIM *lies down,* R. C. *Puts chalk upon face.*)

PHELIM. I'm dead! Shovel the ground all over me! Say, Dutchy, see that my grave's painted green, will you?

(*Enter* BRIDGET, C. D.   CARL *begins to cry*.)

BRIDGET.   Well, what's the matter wid you now? Where's my kisses?
CARL.   Look at your feet!   Look at your feet!
BRIDGET.   What's the matter with my feet?
CARL.   On the ground. Your feet is on the ground.
BRIDGET.   (*sees* PHELIM) Murder!   What's this?
CARL.   He's shooted!   There's an Irish angel in heaven. (*She kneels beside* PHELIM.)
BRIDGET.   My poor, darling, dead Phelim!   How natural he looks!   Did you see him die?   What were his last words?
CARL.   He said, If you ever see Bridget tell her I'll meet her in another world.
PHELIM.   What a Dutch liar!
BRIDGET. (*cries*) I knew he wouldn't forget me! Oh, Carl, my poor heart is breaking!   I'm a widow before I'm married!   Poor man!   He went crazy about me, and now he's dead and will never move again!

(*As she is crying to* CARL, CARL *puts his arms around her to soothe her*.   PHELIM *looks up*.)

CARL.   Oh, I wouldn't cry about him.   He ain't worth it. He ain't the only ace in de pack. It's a good thing he's dead.
PHELIM.   (*aside*) You Dutch villain, I'll murder you. (CARL *slyly kicks* PHELIM.)
CARL. (*aside*) Shut up! You're dead! Stay dead.   (*To* BRIDGET.) Lay your head on the bosom of a handsomer man.   Ah! Bridget! Let me console you.   You are just the kind of a woman that would suit me.   (*Embraces her and kicks* PHELIM *who is sitting up and threatening* CARL *with motions, etc*.   BRIDGET *turns as she speaks and discovers* PHELIM *in a different position.   She screams with astonishment*.)
BRIDGET.   Look there! Look there! He's lying different.
CARL.   Certainly.   He's an awful liar.   He'd lie all the time.   You see, crazy people get all twisted up when they die, and the first thing you know he'll be all tied up in a knot.   Let him lay there, and de crows will eat him up.
BRIDGET.   No! I'll have him buried.   I'll run and get a grave-digger and at the same time make arrangements for our marriage.   (PHELIM *changes again*.)   See! It's turned around again!
CARL.   The Irish die hard.   They've got nine lives like

a cat. But he's dead for the last time. Oh! my darling! Kiss your little chickabiddy on de lip. Oh! my dear wife that is to be. (*Business of kissing her, and* PHELIM *yells "Break away" and lies flat.* BRIDGET *turns and notes position.*)

BRIDGET. Now, then, wait for me here, and we'll have him buried and you'll be my husband as quick as the work can be done. (*Starts to go* R. I E. CARL *calls to her.*)

CARL. One more sweet kiss!

(BRIDGET *runs to his arms, hugs him and starts off* R., *and then turns and comes to him again. This is done to enable* PHELIM *to partially rise and throw himself flat again as* BRIDGET *returns. This is done several times and* BRIDGET *runs out* R. I E., CARL *bidding her to "hurry," etc. Soon as she is out* PHELIM *jumps to his feet in great anger.*)

PHELIM. So I'm dead, am I! I'll feed the worms, will I! (*Produces revolver.*)

CARL. Go get buried! You don't cut any ice-cream around here any more.

PHELIM. I'll show you whether I do or not. There'll be a Dutch angel climbing up to the clouds. (*Fires at* CARL, *who yells and hops as if shot in the foot. Short and funny chase around stage.* CARL *runs off* L. U. E. BRIDGET *returns* R. I E. *and meets* PHELIM C. *She screams.*)

BRIDGET. His ghost! his ghost! (*And scampers off, fainting and screaming,* R. I E. PHELIM *tumbles backward from sudden meeting, and he scampers off* L. I E.)

(*Music. Several shots fired outside of the hotel.* VALDEZ, JASPER, LOPEZ *and guerrillas enter* L., *with* ELINORA *and* RICHARD, *prisoners, door,* C.)

VALDEZ. A very clever ruse, and it succeeded admirably. We have captured the town. Your late prisoners are now your masters. The American dies first.

ELINORA. No—no—spare his life. 'Twas I who am to blame for his participation in these matters. Let me be the one to suffer. Release him and take my life. See, I kneel to you! (*Kneels.*)

RICHARD. Arise! Kneel to no one, save Heaven. Kneel not to a craven cowardly dog for a million lives.

ELINORA. Harken not to him, Roderigo Valdez, but listen to my pleadings for his life.

VALDEZ. Then you love this meddling American!

ELINORA. I do; I do love him!

VALDEZ. Enough! No power on earth could save him now. The message you sent to General Gomez will fail of its mission, as I have a band in ambush to receive the patriots when they come this way!

ELINORA. Will nothing tempt you to release this man?

VALDEZ. No. There is a deeper reason than his interference why I should destroy him. Lopez, take a squad of men with you to the court-yard and convey the American to a spot where I see you from the window. At my signal, shoot to kill!

RICHARD. Cowardly dog! This murder will be avenged tenfold. Farewell, Elinora. (*Crosses to her.*) Remember your mission is to avenge your father and the one who loved you so devotedly.

ELINORA. No, no! They must not take you from me. Richard, my own, I cannot bear to lose you now! (*Clings to him.*)

VALDEZ. Take him away! (LOPEZ *and a soldier take* RICHARD *from her, while one takes her,* R.)

RICHARD. Elinora! Remember! Avenge me if you can. (*He is taken off,* C. D., *by* LOPEZ *and soldiers.*)

ELINORA. (*aside,* R. C.) If I can but gain time the relief party may arrive.

VALDEZ. Once before I gave you a chance which you spurned. I know your motives and see through your disguise and purpose.

ELINORA. I seek the false friend who murdered my father and robbed me of my inheritance.

VALDEZ. You will never find him! Yet I may say this to you: Here is a package of documents relating to that estate, and I hold them out to you as a tempting bait. (*Holds out papers.*) What would you give to possess them?

ELINORA. This is my answer. (*Seizes the papers.*)

VALDEZ. Give me those documents!

ELINORA. When I am dead you can take them from the hand which now holds them! They are mine, and I will die defending them to the last.

VALDEZ. This is quite theatrical, I must say. Your lover is beyond with guns leveled at his breast, my men awaiting the signal to fire. Quite dramatic, is it not? And you—well, you know the fate of a spy. The papers you hold may give you a momentary pleasure, but you are doomed. One chance yet remains. Become mine, and I spare the American! Quick—choose.

ELINORA. I prefer death. And I am sure that Richard Carson would rather die than see me wedded to a coward, a villain, a murderer such as you are!

VALDEZ. These words to me! It is your last threat! (*As he speaks he advances toward her, holding up his hand. She seizes his hand, screams as she beholds the mark in the palm of his hand.*)

ELINORA. There is the brand I have sought! The mark of the murderer which I saw on that fatal night. You—you—Roderigo Valdez—you are the assassin!

VALDEZ. Curses on the mark! I wished to hide it forever from your gaze.

ELINORA. 'Twas you, false wretch, who destroyed my father, and cast me upon the world—penniless, friendless and homeless—while you enjoyed my inheritance! Villain! Traitor! We are face to face at last!

VALDEZ. You have spoken your death-sentence, and Richard Carson's as well. You have discovered my secret, but you will not live to tell it. Blindfold her! (*A man steps forward to blindfold her.*)

ELINORA. Stop! I refuse to be blindfolded. I wish to gaze with my dying glances upon brave Spaniards who can shoot a helpless woman!

VALDEZ. Do not listen to her idle talk—do as I command! Blindfold her, and shoot the spy!

ELINORA. Stay! You and your murderous associates may fire upon me, but I reserve the right to die under the colors I have loved, fought for, and wish to embrace in my dying moments. (*She places a Cuban flag which she produces from her bosom upon her shoulders*) This flag has been consecrated by the blood of Cuban patriots! Fire upon it, and add another stain to the credit of Spain! Here is another emblem (*takes out American flag, places it over heart*) Fire upon this if you dare!

VALDEZ. Am I to be baffled by a weak girl and her senseless talk? Up with your guns and fire upon her. Why do you hesitate?

JASPER. Captain, I for one will not shoot down a woman in cold blood! I may be a villain, but I draw the line at that, and I absolutely refuse to obey any such order!

VALDEZ. Am I awake or dreaming? Jasper refusing to remove a human being for our own safety? What does it mean?

JASPER. It means that no matter how vile or utterly lost a man may be, there is some good in him yet remaining. I have a sister at home, and I would kill the man that in-

sulted or threatened her life. As I wish my sister to be
treated, so will I treat this helpless girl—spy or no spy !

(*Bugle call heard in distance.* ELINORA *screams.*)

ELINORA.   The bugle !   General Gomez is at hand. My
prayer has been answered.

VALDEZ.   I'll give the signal !

(*Music.*   VALDEZ *rushes to window as* PHELIM *and* CARL
show themselves at window and fire. VALDEZ *staggers,
tries to reach* ELINORA *to shoot her, but falls dead at her
feet.* PHELIM *and* CARL *come through window and attempt to strike down* JASPER, *but* ELINORA *protects him.*
RICHARD *and* LOPEZ *enter,* D. C. *Sword combat.* LOPEZ
*disarmed and overpowered. Guerrillas driven on and over-
powered by Cubans. One hands flag to* ELINORA, *which
she waves in triumph.* SOPHIE *and* BRIDGET *enter* L. 1 E.
PHELIM *drops on his knees between them, begging for
mercy,* L. C. RICHARD *and* ELINORA, C.)

CURTAIN

www.ingramcontent.com/pod-product-compliance
Lightning Source LLC
Chambersburg PA
CBHW022040080426
42733CB00007B/906